REVELATION

ALSO BY DENNIS COVINGTON

Redneck Riviera: Armadillos, Outlaws, and the Demise of an American Dream

Cleaving: The Story of a Marriage (with Vicki Covington)

Salvation on Sand Mountain: Snake Handling and Redemption in Southern Appalachia

Lasso the Moon

Lizard

REVELATION

A Search for Faith in a Violent Religious World

DENNIS COVINGTON

Little, Brown and Company

New York   Boston   London

Little, Brown and Company
Hachette Book Group
1290 Avenue of the Americas, New York, NY 10104
littlebrown.com

First Edition: February 2016

Little, Brown and Company is a division of Hachette Book Group, Inc.
The Little, Brown name and logo are trademarks of Hachette Book Group, Inc.

The publisher is not responsible for websites (or their content) that are not owned by the publisher.

The Hachette Speakers Bureau provides a wide range of authors for speaking events. To find out more, go to hachettespeakersbureau.com or call (866) 376-6591.

Portions of this work have appeared in different form in the *New York Times, Confrontation, Image,* and *Iron Horse Literary Review.* The full article from the *Times* has been used with permission, as have the much smaller pieces from the other publications, all with my deepest gratitude.

This is a work of nonfiction, but memory is an imperfect tool.

ISBN 978-0-316-36861-2

LCCN 2015954873

10 9 8 7 6 5 4 3 2 1

RRD-C

Printed in the United States of America

In memory of
Sam Scott Covington Jr. (1934–1994),
my brother

CONTENTS

CONTENTS

Arise, cry out in the night: in the beginning of the watches pour out thine heart like water before the face of the Lord: lift up thy hands toward him for the life of thy young children, that faint for hunger in the top of every street.

—Lamentations 2:19

REVELATION

AUTHOR'S NOTE

The names of all people in this book who are not public figures have been changed to protect their privacy, given that they often live in places consumed by violence.

Prologue

On a star-filled night in March of 2014, I was driving west from Lubbock, Texas, to Prescott, Arizona, where I hoped to find the whereabouts of Carl and Marsha Mueller, the parents of Kayla Mueller, a twenty-five-year-old humanitarian aid worker who had been kidnapped by the Islamic State of Iraq and al-Sham seven months before.

The public did not yet know that an American woman was among the Western hostages held by ISIS, the most brutal terrorist organization in the world. But along the Turkish-Syrian border, I had met, by chance, a man who claimed to be Kayla's husband. He was Syrian. He'd freely given me the information that his American wife was in an ISIS prison. He said they'd been kidnapped together in Aleppo, Syria, in August, but that he'd been able to escape their captors. It was extremely important that what he'd told me be kept secret, he added.

When I had dinner with the Syrian a few months later, he said he'd been imprisoned again, but had escaped or been released. The circumstances were unclear to me. He also said he was in contact with Kayla's parents in Arizona. I asked if they might be willing to talk to me. I told him I was writing a book about faith, and about the strange confluence of faith and violence — or at least religion and violence — around the world. I wanted to ask the Muellers how they were managing to hold up under what seemed to me to be the worst possible circumstances for any parent of any child.

When he told me they'd be willing to talk, I left the Turkish-Syrian border, flew to Texas, rented a car, and headed to Arizona. From what I'd found on the Internet, the Muellers' address and phone number were out of date. I avoided calling Kayla's husband to get the current contact information, and I ignored a message from him asking for clarification about my intentions. I didn't trust him. I couldn't understand how he had managed to escape ISIS twice while Kayla had remained imprisoned. And I didn't believe that he was her husband. I wanted to talk to Kayla's parents directly, not through him anymore.

He wasn't the father of a daughter. I was the father of two. They were close to Kayla's age, twenty-six and twenty-eight, and they were the most precious people on earth to me. I thought that Kayla's parents would understand that we had a connection through our love for our daughters, and that they might open up to me, even if they feared I would violate their trust. That was my hope, anyway.

In the car with me that night was a photocopied article I'd retrieved from the Internet about Kayla's visit back home during the spring before her kidnapping. She'd given a talk to her father's Kiwanis Club about her work with refugees along the Turkish-Syrian border. The Kiwanis Club is an international service organization dedicated to the children of the world. Kayla was standing in front of the Kiwanis logo, and to her right, in the background, was an unfurled American flag.

Looking at Kayla's radiant and self-assured smile in the photo, I knew how proud her parents must have been of her. I could also imagine how concerned they must have been for her safety when she returned to the Middle East.

Could imagine... could imagine. What inadequate words these were, given what the Muellers must have been going through that night as I wound my way toward them.

The stretch of interstate from Santa Rosa to Clines Corners, New Mexico, was sparsely populated, the kind of place I liked. When I'd first moved to Texas, I'd been bankrupt and living with my younger daughter in an abandoned farmhouse on the edge of a canyon, fifty miles from the university where I taught. It was the flattest place on earth and one of the happiest times of my life.

At night, we'd go outside at various hours to note how the universe had revolved slowly around our heads. The Big Dipper turned on its own axis. The Milky Way, that terrifying river of light, stayed intact. But the constellations were always in motion, imperceptible unless one had been rigorous in observation and kept track. Where we lived then, unlike at any place I'd lived before, it was possible to do just that.

The only sources of competing light were from a ranch house a mile away in one direction, and another ranch house a mile and a half away in the opposite direction. There were no other artificial lights as far as the horizon. We were living in a nocturnal paradise, or at least it seemed that way to me.

My spiritual life, on the other hand, was a mess. I was in the middle of my fifties, with more broken promises to God than I could ever name. I'd been baptized at birth into a Methodist family in Alabama and been saved by grace at the age of sixteen. Then I'd backslid into a fallen state for almost twenty years, until I sobered up, started a family, and tried to serve the Lord.

In my forties, after covering the trial of a snake-handling preacher convicted of attempting to murder his wife with rattlesnakes, I wrote *Salvation on Sand Mountain,* a book about my journey with the handlers. I briefly became one myself. I even considered being baptized by a snake-handling preacher in the Tennessee River before opting instead for baptism in our sedate, urban Baptist church back in Birmingham. But I ultimately defied the Baptist doctrine of "once saved, always saved" by falling from grace yet again while writing a second book, this time a joint memoir with my wife, Vicki Covington.

That book was to be about our search for what Jesus had called "living water," the kind he'd offered to the Samaritan woman at Jacob's well, the kind that could wash away her sins and forever slake her thirst. We thought we could find this spiritual water by leading a team from our church to hand-drill a well to literal water in a desperately poor village in El Salvador.

We did drill the well, but the problem, by then, was that Vicki and I had fallen in love with other people, so our book about spiritual renewal became instead a confession of sin without the requisite plea for forgiveness at the end.

So much for my claim to godliness. Our book *Cleaving* was honest, yes, but that honesty had come at the expense of the people we loved the most.

When I was asked to step aside from my leadership role in the church, I didn't think my church had failed me. I knew I'd failed my church. But I didn't feel as though God had turned his back on me. Not at all. I felt he was the only thing that kept me going during those difficult times. He seemed to have been expecting that I was going to mess things up.

So I figured my inability to "rest assured" in church must have been man-made—the result of doctrine, dogma, a regimen of oft-repeated beliefs, as though the very recitation of them could somehow fill the dark hole at the center of my heart. Instead, I found solace in the definition of faith in Hebrews 11:1 as a "substance" that could be sought out and found. And James 2:26 became my mantra: "For as the body without the spirit is dead, so faith without works is dead also."

I began to reimagine faith as an action rather than a set of beliefs, as something that anyone, believer or not, could initiate if only given the time and the means. I was no longer physically able to hand-drill a water well, but I could still write, so in my sixties I decided to do what Jesus expected his disciples to do when he asked them to go as witnesses to his suffering on the Cross. I decided to go to places where people were subject to extremity, as his followers like Saint Peter and Saint Paul had been, and as the generations that came after them would be, the ones who'd be "mocked, imprisoned, stoned, sawn asunder, tempted, and slain with the sword."

In this quest, I might find pilgrims who'd taken a similar path, people like Kayla Mueller, who had said: "Some people find God in church, some people find God in nature, some people find God in love, I find God in suffering."

After I'd gassed up that night at a service station in Moriarty, New Mexico, I drove due north till I'd left the artificial lights behind. On the shoulder of the two-lane blacktop, I stopped, got out of the car, waited for my eyes to adjust, and then took in the whole night sky. My dog and I did this same thing twice a night, but the sky was better in this part of New Mexico than it was above my newly rented farmhouse in Texas, which was too close to the city for me to see the Milky Way.

Each constellation in that sky in New Mexico was chiseled, as if from ice. And there was one bright light in the western sky that I could not name for the life of me. I'd looked for it before in my stargazers' book, and I knew I'd have to look again when I got back to Texas. That night, though, I just took the bright light in the western sky as a sign that Kayla Mueller surely would be coming home.

1

Easter in Juárez

Now faith is the substance of things hoped for, the evidence of things not seen.

—Hebrews 11:1

My search for faith in a violent religious world began in a most unlikely place—the parking lot of a Cajun café in Lubbock, Texas, in the spring of 2012, on a day so hot the prairie dogs had refused to come out of their burrows and a red-tailed hawk was resigned to harassing housecats at the construction site across the highway from where I sat.

I was waiting in the parking lot to meet writer Charles Bowden for the first time. He had driven up from Las Cruces, New Mexico, to give a talk that night at the university. His most recent book, *Murder City*, had been about the drug war in Juárez, Mexico, at that time the most dangerous city in the world. Chuck and his colleague Molly Molloy had also recently coedited a book titled *El Sicario: The Autobiography of a Mexican Assassin,* a monologue stitched together from interviews they had done with a cartel hit man who'd found Christ and was willing to confess his crimes in excruciating detail. This reformed hit man used to "dismember and bathe people in acid while keeping them alive via adrenaline shots just to torture them a bit more."

In her introduction to the book, Molly said of El Sicario, "I believe he is convinced that we are part of a fraternity of holy fools that God has placed on his path. He believes that God has a purpose for his life, that part of this purpose is fulfilled by telling his story, and that Bowden and I are tools to make it happen."

A car with New Mexico plates pulled into the parking space ahead of me, and a tall man in a khaki-colored ball cap got out. I caught up with him at the café door.

"Chuck," I said. "How was your trip?"

"Fine. I can't complain." We shook hands, and I followed him inside.

The place was almost empty. Bowden chose a table near the bar, and I sat down across from him, facing the street. The waitress, not one of my students, brought us iced tea and coffee. She was wearing pressed jeans and a purple tank top. Bowden and I studied the menus, and although I recommended the gumbo, he ordered two eggs over easy with hash browns.

When the waitress was out of earshot, I told him I'd loved *Murder City*, even though it had given me the willies.

He nodded.

"Particularly what happened to Miss Sinaloa," I said. In the book, he'd reported that a former beauty queen had been gang-raped by Mexican soldiers or police. Lost her mind because of that.

But this time Bowden didn't respond. Maybe I'd touched a nerve. I said: "Sorry it's so hot in here."

He leaned back and lifted his tea glass like a semaphore. "Nothing compared to New Mexico," he said. I knew from the book jacket that he was older than I was, sixty-seven or so: a good man, from everything I'd read, but more soft-spoken than I'd expected. His voice over the phone had been gravelly and strong.

When the waitress brought our food, we settled in to eat. That's when I noticed the design on his ball cap. It was a khaki star with "WW II" embossed in script above it, and "Korea" in script underneath.

"I didn't know you were in Korea." I ran the calculation in my head and still didn't see how that could be possible.

"I wasn't in Korea," he said. "I was in World War Two."

"Good God. How old are you?"

"Eighty-four."

"Eighty-four? How do you manage to do all that crazy running around in Juárez?"

"I'm retired."

"Retired from *what?*"

That's when my cell phone rang. It was Bowden's number. "Where are you?" he said.

I glanced across the table at the old man in the veteran's cap. "I'm at the Cajun restaurant. Where are you?"

"I'm sitting at the bar right behind you." Then he appeared at my side and took a seat at the table. He was a tall man all right, with a deep tan and turquoise eyes. "Thanks for the recommendation," he said. "That gumbo was really good." We immediately started talking about the latest violence in Juárez, and the veteran across the table didn't bat an eye. Then an artist friend of Bowden's joined us— Alice Leora Briggs—and there was more talk, this time about the former cartel hit man Bowden had come to admire.

Outside on the sidewalk, Bowden told me he'd read one of my books and liked it. When he asked about my current project, I told him I was heading to the site of ancient Antioch on a search for faith as it was defined in the book of Hebrews. Bowden said he didn't believe in any of that religious crap, but he had an idea. "You ought to head down to Juárez," he said. "There's something spiritual going on down there, and I'd like to know what you make of it."

This wasn't the first time I'd been on the verge of a spiritual quest and someone had pointed me in an unexpected direction. When I was a soldier in the early 1970s, I'd agreed to do volunteer work at the Leesville State School for Retarded Boys in Louisiana. There I met a disfigured thirteen-year-old boy who wouldn't speak, but who could sing hymns so beautifully, my knees buckled in gratitude to whomever had allowed me to witness that. In the 1980s, I'd been to a war in El Salvador, and that experience had literally sobered me up. Then in Alabama in the 1990s, while covering an attempted murder trial involving a snake-handling preacher, I'd discovered the power of the Holy Ghost, something that had only been talked about in the staid churches of my childhood. That power was dangerous, as evidenced by the rattlesnakes, so my family was relieved when I came to my senses, but I'd learned that the physical senses were ephemeral; the spiritual ones might be the only ones that lasted forever.

The news Chuck Bowden wanted to share was equally unconventional. He told me that some lunatics were going to burn an effigy of Judas on the day before Easter in front of the cathedral in Juárez. The purpose was to drive Satan out of the city. So on the Thursday before Easter, I drove down to El Paso, the border city on the American side of the Rio Grande. Five police officers had been murdered in Juárez the week before at an off-duty party celebrating their return from a month-long stay, for their own safety, in area hotels. The day I arrived was the day that José Antonio Acosta Hernández, a Mexican drug kingpin thought to be responsible for as many as 1500 deaths, had been sentenced to ten life terms in prison.

Since Mexican judges had been reluctant to try this monster in their own country, he'd been extradited across the river to El Paso, where he'd pleaded guilty in federal court to the 2010 murder of three people with ties to the U.S. Consulate in Juárez. Acosta Hernández, better known as "El Diego," also admitted that he'd ordered the massacre of sixteen Mexican teenagers at a Juárez birthday party and the detonation of a car bomb in the center of downtown that had killed four other innocents. Ten life terms just didn't seem long enough for El Diego, who had headed up La Línea, the vicious enforcement arm of the Juárez cartel. But the U.S. district judge had done her best to match the punishment with the crime. After reading El Diego's sentence aloud, she shipped him off to an undisclosed maximum-security prison, a place from which no one had ever escaped or been paroled.

When Good Friday dawned cool and clear, residents on both sides of the river must have breathed a sigh of relief, but by midmorning, as I walked over the bridge and into Juárez to check the place out, a hot, dry wind had picked up, and the city had begun to settle into its customary paralysis, a resigned veneer of traffic and bus exhaust. Good Friday was an occasion to mark the suffering of Jesus on the Cross, and the penitents at the Church of San Lorenzo would be reminded of their own vulnerability when their prayers during Mass were punctuated by the sound of gunfire. One parishioner was struck by a stray bullet but survived.

Outside, though, a cigarette merchant known as "El Pájaro" was not so fortunate. He had been chatting with his brother in the parking lot of a nearby store when a man in a black minivan pulled up and fired at least five bullets at his head. El Pájaro dropped to his knees and then slumped against a concrete planter. When the gunman realized his target was still alive, he fired twice more. A photograph of El Pájaro would appear the next day on the front page of a Juárez newspaper. In blue jeans, black shirt, and tennis shoes, he would look as though he'd just stopped to tie his shoelaces, but readers of the paper would know he'd never rise up again.

A more promising attempt at resurrection had taken place not far from El Pájaro's neighborhood, where Lorenzo Garza Chávez, a fifty-year-old father, brother, and son, had just been released from the state penitentiary after serving seventeen years behind bars. His aging mother had greeted him at the prison door with hugs and kisses, his sister with a cigarette. And as the three climbed into the family car, he told the women he planned to start a new life, get a good job, and dedicate himself to the welfare of his two sons. But they traveled only one block before stopping at a red light. There, a young man approached the car on foot and shot Lorenzo four times at point-blank range. He died before anybody could get him to the hospital. A nine-year-old boy in a passing car was also hit by a bullet but made it to the hospital in time and survived.

So what was the good news in Juárez on Good Friday? The good news was that a slight decline in the 2011 death toll from the drug war seemed to be continuing into 2012. The bad news was that more than 10,300 people had been murdered in the city during the previous four years. And the slaughter continued. And no one seemed able to make it stop.

The next day, four of us—Chuck, his partner Molly Molloy, a Santa Fe photographer named Monroe Smith, and I—took a grimy city bus high into a neighborhood that clung to the side of a mountain northwest of the city center. Chuck, his hair windblown and his eyes aglow, told me that in other parts of Mexico, the rich had always taken the higher ground for their estates. But in the city of Juárez, where water, sewer, and power lines coursed along the valley floor, the poor lived on the mountainsides without those critical services. "At least they've got a view," he said.

We were headed for lunch at Casa Tabor, the simple home of an American priest and nun, Father Peter Hinde and Sister Betty Campbell, both in their eighties. They had lived among the poor in Latin America for more than thirty years—and always, it seemed, in the most dangerous places: Argentina during the Dirty War, Peru in the days of the Shining Path, and a number of times in El Salvador, where they'd lost more friends than they could count, including Archbishop Oscar Romero and the four American churchwomen: Ita Ford, Maura Clarke, Jean Donovan, and Dorothy Kazel. Portraits of the four, and one of the monsignor, were hanging on the wall. (Our hostess, Sister Betty, was also an artist.)

When I told her I'd been to El Salvador many times, she could hardly contain herself. "This is so Catholic, but I've just got to show you," she said. She disappeared into her bedroom and came out with a locket which, when opened, revealed a small swatch of what looked like gauze, stained by a large, irregular spot. "It's Archbishop Romero's blood," she said. "A nun who was in the chapel when he was assassinated gave it to me." She said she'd had a much larger piece, but that a guest at Casa Tabor had picked it up from an end table and never thought to return it. "That's why I keep this one in my bedroom," Betty concluded with a smile.

She said that Father Peter had founded CRISPAZ (Christians for Peace in El Salvador) while they'd been there, and that he was scheduled to receive an honorary doctorate from Christian Theological Seminary in Indianapolis that very summer, even though he'd never graduated from college, instead joining the Army Air Corps during World War II. He'd begun his life's work in the civil rights era of the 1960s and had been close to Stokely Carmichael and his Black Panther movement.

"Tell them what they called you, Peter," she said.

"Not now." He was deep in conversation with Chuck.

"No, please," Betty said.

"Oh, all right. Lefty."

"And not because of his politics," Betty added.

"They knew I used to play baseball. I pitched left-handed."

So what was Father Peter doing now in Juárez?

Burying the dead.

"Almost everyone asks him to perform the services," Betty said. "He doesn't charge, you know."

"They give me what they can."

And demand for his services, as would be expected in a place like Juárez, was great. He and Betty had not owned a car since 1978. But somehow he managed to make his daily rounds in the neighborhood on foot, goatlike up treacherous paths past frothy raw sewage, roosters, pigs, and the poorest of the city's poor. These were the families that produced the *sicarios* (assassins) and *correos* (errand boys), who were the indispensables in this nightmare war. But most of the residents, he said, were trying to scrape by honestly.

When we took that morning walk with him, he stopped to admire the progress made on a neighbor's house. The man and his son were adding another room for his daughter's family, a room made of unreinforced concrete blocks. During the week these men worked in the *maquiladoras,* the manufacturing plants in free-trade zones made possible by NAFTA, the North American Free Trade Agreement that Chuck hated, primarily because, in his view, the factories treated employees like indentured servants and paid them outrageously low wages. He thought the factory owners and investors were making a killing, and that the cartels were skimming off the top.

Since a bag of cement could cost three days' wages, a home improvement like this room on the neighbor's house might take months. And there was a built-in overhead that everybody paid: "A dollar or a bullet." Either you paid the messenger or your husband or wife or child disappeared, or you and your children were tortured and raped. And even then, as in every business, there were mistakes. Having turned over everything, you still might never see your family again. And did you go to the police? Oh no, that was the worst thing to do. If the police weren't yet on the cartel's payroll, the fear was that they were probably still on the take.

Corruption in Juárez, Chuck said, was like the weather. Rain or shine, it was always there, and it and the drug violence were killing the city.

The meal at Casa Tabor was simple: lentil soup, salad, and bread. I shared the blessing in Spanish that a friend in the Dominican Republic had taught me. Chuck and his companions brought out a bottle of wine and cake. Afterward we toured the backyard, its dirt raked clean. Betty introduced us to her dog and chickens, and showed us her raised vegetable bed. She pointed out the labyrinth she and Peter had formed out of mounds of dirt. There were two chairs that would be used for contemplation after we'd found our way out. And on the wall of a covered patio in back were colorful panels that Betty had illustrated. Underneath the illustrations were lists of the city's dead, and on a table were computer printouts of thousands of other names that needed to be added. They were categorized according to male and female, missing or confirmed dead. She handed us pens. "You can add a few names to the panels, if you'd like."

So we did. And then we explained that we'd better be going. We had to be at the Plaza de Armas, which fronted the cathedral in the center of town, by six.

"What's happening there?" Peter asked.

"The lunatics from the asylum are burning Judas in order to drive Satan out of the city," Chuck said.

Peter smiled, but Betty was not amused. "I don't approve of that."

"Well, Pastor wants us there," Chuck said.

She shook her head. "Not me."

"Nor I," Peter said, but he looked as though he might like to go.

Molly Molloy was walking beside me. "A lot of the truck drivers, prostitutes, and drug dealers worship Santa Muerte," she was saying.

"It's a branch of Catholicism," Chuck whispered, "an adjunct. Like carrying a rabbit foot."

Fortunately, Father Peter hadn't heard that exchange. "I'll walk you to the bus stop," he said. "You can't be too careful in this neighborhood. And please don't photograph the drug houses that we pass on the way."

In this manner, we found ourselves in the very heart of Juárez. Because it was the day before Easter, the Plaza de Armas was packed with extended families, juggling clowns, men costumed like Montezuma and his warriors, and ice cream, soft drink, and tamale vendors.

"Don't let this fool you," Chuck said. "The only happy people in Juárez are the lunatics at the asylum."

There were street preachers on nearly every corner, but no one seemed to be paying attention to them. On the bandstand in the center of the park, though, was an enormous and very odd portrait of Jesus and the Devil. They were arm wrestling, and that *did* attract stares and comments.

As I stood there taking in the atmosphere, I remembered reading a newspaper article by John MacCormack, a San Antonio reporter who had met two young photographers at this very park. The young men had just gotten jobs with *El Diario*, the local paper. They were excited to have their press credentials, and they promised to meet up again with the older reporter later that afternoon. About two hours after the young men left the plaza, MacCormack got word that the two had been ambushed by cartel hit men. One of them had died instantly, a bullet to his head. The other played dead until the men sped away, and then he crawled to safety, injured but alive. I wondered if all this had happened on a day like today.

Chuck nudged me with his elbow when a busload of what must have been the lunatics he'd been talking about pulled up, and he introduced me to the wild-haired ex-addict and ex-con who'd brought them there. The man's given name was José Antonio Galván, but the patients just called him Pastor, as would we. Pastor was dressed all in black, like a Mexican Johnny Cash hopped up on the Holy Ghost. After his time as a radio evangelist and street preacher, he had decided to dedicate his life to the city's dispossessed. He'd also boxed, played the guitar, and lately taken up oil painting. That was his canvas of Jesus and Satan arm wrestling that overlooked us from the railing of the bandstand in the park.

Pastor showed us the papier-mâché Judas he'd brought with him, which he'd made himself from local newspaper articles with photos of dismembered bodies dumped in ravines. He'd painted over the photos with thick red paint, and he'd given Judas a devil's horns, goatee, and tail. A cigarette butt was stuffed into Judas's mouth, and attached to his body were empty beer cans, plastic syringes, bags of white powder that looked like cocaine, and something organic that resembled Acapulco Gold. Also attached to the effigy were prescription bottles, firecrackers, and unrolled condoms. My eye was drawn to the pair of black panties Judas wore.

"What's that represent?" I asked.

"Prostitution," Pastor said. "Promiscuity, and men with men." He clapped my shoulder and looked deep into my eyes. "God bless you for coming down here, brother. The Lord's got plans for you."

As Pastor greeted others he recognized in the park, Chuck told me the narcos didn't know what to make of him. "They don't think he's a crook."

But El Sicario, the hit man turned Christian that Chuck and Molly had interviewed, thought Pastor would be killed if he kept pushing his luck by not paying cartel hit men for protection.

After a rabid little street preacher in too-tight boots had warmed up the crowd, Pastor took the microphone and preached himself hoarse until twilight fell and the pigeons began to roost in the bandstand eaves. Many of the hundred or so asylum patients had not been able to come, but he laid hands on the ones who had, in order to heal their infirmities. He accompanied their singing on his battered guitar. And after the effigy of Judas had been strung up between two trees, Pastor did what he had come there to do. He ordered Satan out of the city and called for gasoline.

We scrambled to fill squirt bottles and then used lighters and rolled-up newspapers to set Judas afire. The old boy was slow to catch because of that coat of red paint, but after a while he burst into flame, and at what sounded like gunfire the pigeons took flight. We dove for cover. "It's just firecrackers!" Pastor shouted after us. We'd forgotten about those, and when we'd reassembled in front of the bandstand, Pastor ordered the smoldering Judas lowered to the ground. The first patient to stomp on the effigy was an intense woman in a canvas fishing cap. She was shaking a purple tambourine as she stomped. Monroe Smith, the photographer, told me she'd once killed a man over a cigarette. "That's why I always take a fresh pack with me when I visit the asylum," he said.

As the smoke from the effigy cleared, another wild-eyed patient I'll call Dante and two young girls in spotless Easter dresses, bystanders until then, began dancing on Judas's charred remains.

Chuck nudged me. "So what do you think?"

What I was thinking about at that moment was the print of *The Peaceable Kingdom* that hung on the wall of my childhood Sunday school class: the lion with the antelope, the wolf lying down with the lambs. Dante was the lion or the wolf; the girls, the antelopes or lambs.

But Chuck just nodded toward Dante as he stomped the ashes and said, "He beat one of the other patients to death."

After a day like that, my mind often worked frantically in sleep. Even my dreams were like being awake. In one, in particular, I heard my cell phone ring. I didn't get to it in time to answer the call, but the name that popped up was Luke. I didn't think I'd ever met anyone named Luke: I knew I didn't have a friend with that name. So the next morning, when I woke with a start, I picked up my phone to check it again. No one had called me the night before or that morning, and of course there was no one named Luke on my contacts list. So I did that impulsive, superstitious thing that believers, and sometimes even nonbelievers, might be prone to do. I retrieved the Bible the Gideons had planted in the drawer of my bedside table and let it fall open. And yes, it opened to Luke, and the first verses my eyes fell upon were the ones Jesus had uttered as he was bearing the weight of his cross on the way to Calvary:

[28]But Jesus turning unto them said, Daughters of Jerusalem, weep not for me, but weep for yourselves, and for your children.

[29]For, behold, the days are coming, in the which they shall say, Blessed are the barren, and the wombs that never bare, and the paps which never gave suck.

[30]Then shall they begin to say to the mountains, Fall on us; and to the hills, Cover us.

[31]For if they do these things in a green tree, what shall be done in the dry?

I e-mailed Chuck about that experience and included the passage from Luke. Although not a believer, he responded seriously and passed the e-mail along to Molly.

When I got back to Lubbock, Chuck sent me an e-mail with an attached photo of nine bound and hooded dead men hanging from an overpass in Nuevo Laredo, a town six hundred miles downriver from Juárez. He said he figured Pastor had succeeded in driving Satan out of Juárez, but that the residents of Nuevo Laredo probably had a bone to pick with us now that Satan had moved in with them.

A few days later, more remains of twelve young women were discovered in the desert outside Juárez. The month's death toll was still running behind the previous month's, a sign, according to the *El Paso Times,* that things were improving on the Mexican side of the river. Those more than ten thousand dead in Juárez over the past four years had mostly been young to middle-aged males associated with the drug trade. But these young women in the desert appeared to have been between the ages of fifteen and nineteen. Forensic technicians at the scene speculated they'd been tortured and raped before death.

The younger dead girls were identified sooner than the older ones, and Chuck told me that Sister Betty was comforting the mothers of the dead. He was clearly moved by this. Despite his friendship with Pastor, Father Peter, and Sister Betty, though, he reminded me that he was not a believer. "You know I can't abide creeds and priests," he said, "and the very notion turns me into Voltaire. But I cannot fathom people who think life is meaningless. The fucking dog at my feet knows better than that."

The fucking dog at my feet knows better than that.

I knew then I'd stepped into the presence of something beyond belief. The conviction that life has meaning, I thought, must be the place where faith begins.

2

Seven Days in May

At 6:15 this morning two heads and four hands were found in the parking lot of a nightclub called Bandoleros located on Avenue Technologico just meters from Boulevard Zaragoza in Juárez. The heads and hands were unidentified by authorities, who estimated they belonged to two males between the ages of 25 and 30. Along with the heads, crime technicians found a white bucket and at least two empty black plastic bags. Authorities have launched a search operation for the bodies corresponding to the heads. They hope during the next few hours to identify the two murdered men and establish the cause of death for both of them.
    —*El Diario*, Ciudad Juárez, May 14, 2012

Pastor had two offices in Juárez, both with adjoining bedrooms. One was in the headquarters of his charity, Vision in Action. The bed was king-sized with a colorful, thick comforter. He said I could nap there anytime I happened to be in town. There was a life-sized coat of armor by his desk in the office, in clear reference to Ephesians 6:11: "Put on the whole armour of God, that ye may be able to stand against the wiles of the devil."

A speed bag hung from the ceiling in one of the corners of Pastor's office. He happily demonstrated his prowess with it, and given the location and nature of his work, I figured the boxing idea was a good one. The office was turquoise and stood catty-corner from a rarely open *lavandería*. I understood, without being told, that this was a very bad neighborhood, but everyone at the office said the same thing anyway with a smile. The office was close to a Home Depot, Pastor added, as though that indicated something positive about property values, until he remembered the kid who'd been gunned down in the store's parking lot just the other day. Despite its location, the door of Vision in Action was never locked while I was there. It simply had a sign on it that read "This property is protected by Jesus Christ."

Three staff members worked at the office, including a handyman who was my age and had seen it all. It surprised me when I heard him talk about the violence in Juárez in a matter-of-fact way. Perhaps that was because the violence was so *much* a matter of fact.

Pastor couldn't wait to take me on a real tour of the neighborhood, he said, and within a four-square-block area, he showed me just about all I wanted to see. The first spot was a street corner on a major boulevard where four men had been killed—machine-gunned, it looked like from the pock marks in the bricks, with no effort made to keep a tight shot pattern. A block away was the garage where three male bodies had been dumped, semiclothed and castrated, Pastor said. Around the corner from that site, three more guys had been lined up against a wall and executed. And a block farther, on the other side of the street, was the house where a pair of government ministers had been murdered, their offices torched. Pastor hoped they were already dead by the time the fire got to them. They'd had bodyguards, he added, but maybe the guards had been in on the hit. Oh, and one more place, he said, ushering me along. See all the broken glass and bullet holes? he asked. He didn't know whether anyone had died there, though. It was across the street from a school, from which we heard the sound of piano scales accompanied by a young female voice.

I told him I'd recently read about some heads in a parking lot. "Sure," he said. "I can take you there." So he drove me to Bandoleros, where the two heads and four hands had been found, rather neatly arranged, judging from the photos in *El Diario*. One of the heads in the photos was still wearing a blindfold.

"Imagine the pain," Pastor said, and he shook his own head.

The woman who was executed inside her house in Colonia Azteca Saturday afternoon was an agent in the Public Prosecutor's Office

for more than 15 years and was assigned to the State Police, Preventive Division. Her son also died in the attack. He had been released from prison after serving time for the murder of a federal agent in a bar in 2010.
— *El Diario*, Ciudad Juárez, May 13, 2012

Pastor's other office was at the lunatic asylum, more properly known as a refuge for the mentally incapacitated, which seemed to emerge from the desert outside Juarez like a walled fortress on the plains of southern Spain. There was a white bus with a smashed windshield outside, and a green van without a tag. Blankets and serapes were hung out to dry from barbed wire in front of the chicken and pig pens, and stray dogs lounged in whatever shade they could find. When we pulled to a stop, Dante, the pear-shaped man who had beat another patient to death, wrapped his arms around me before I could even get out of the car.

"He's a good boy now," Pastor said.

The asylum project had begun in 1998 when Pastor started taking people in off the streets of Juárez, the ones nobody else dared care for, the human refuse, he said, of the city. At first they huddled among blankets in concrete-block cells with matted straw roofs. That's what it had been like when Chuck Bowden and photographer Julian Cardona had stumbled across the place while looking for a mountain-sized piece of narco art commissioned by the Juárez cartel boss, Amado Carrillo.

Chuck was the one who had brought the world's attention, and no little money, to Pastor's project. By the time I arrived, the asylum was a fully operational facility with a walled but unlocked courtyard; an enormous cistern for the water brought by a tank truck from the city every Monday; and a kitchen that served three basic meals a day. The flies that carpeted every surface of the screened porch where patients sliced fruits and vegetables were the least of the asylum's worries. With more than a hundred in residence and only a few full-time staff, it was up to the patients themselves to wash their blankets and clothes in an enormous tub in the courtyard and to bathe, groom, and even sometimes restrain or medicate one another.

Those unable to help in this way were cared for by the rest. The ones who acted out violently, a quarter of them at any one time, might be locked in barred cells, sometimes for as long as a month or two. "Don't go into any of the cells," Pastor said emphatically. A terrible incident had occurred when a cat wandered into one that was occupied by a severely disabled older woman. Somehow she had crucified the animal against the bars, then gouged out its eyes and eaten them.

Dante had to be watched very carefully, but he was certainly affectionate with me, and a personal favorite of Pastor. And that murder was the only time the police had shown up at the asylum. Pastor said they took one look at Dante and refused to take him to jail. "You keep him," they said. "He's crazy."

The woman who had once killed a man over a cigarette was bipolar, Pastor said, and could change in an instant. The staff had a nickname for her, "Crazy Baby," a moniker she was proud of. Her job in the asylum was to brush everyone's teeth. She also cleaned the staff's rooms. In fact, she was the only patient who had access to the section of the facility where Pastor had his office and bedroom. This was a thought never far from my mind because that was the bedroom where I was sleeping every night.

The large office space that adjoined the bedroom also served as Pastor's art studio. He was extravagant with color and primitive in execution. But the power of his work was inescapable, and the motifs were right out of the people and places he knew best, the Juárez subculture of poverty and neglect, and the political and religious hierarchy that was both sustaining and killing it. His largest and most controversial canvas was called *La Casa del Diablo*. It was a painting of the cathedral in the center of the city where we'd burned the effigy of Judas. In the painting an enormous red-and-black-winged demon appears to be swooping down from one of the cathedral's towers. The demon is carrying a woman in its claws. She's wearing a traditional dress in the colors of the Mexican flag, and there's a dahlia, the national flower, in her hair. She appears to be dead.

There are bones scattered all over the park in front of the cathedral. Graves and skulls. In the foreground the scene is watched by a border patrol officer with binoculars, a voyeur just like us.

Three men and a woman were shot to death this morning in a house in the neighborhood of Puente del Bravo. A woman in search of her son, Jorge, arrived at the house only to discover that he was one of the dead. A 7-year-old boy was also injured in the attack.
—El Diario, Ciudad Juárez, May 26, 2012

I came to know the patients briefly and superficially during my week at the asylum, but they gave me gifts that I can hardly put into words. Lety and Elia, for instance, were sisters who had been chained like dogs since they were babies and then abandoned by their addict parents. One of the sisters, now in her thirties, could not speak and was very shy. The other could say a few words and loved to wash dishes, and whenever I saw her in the courtyard, she would run up and greet me with a smile and a hug. Others shared verses of Scripture they'd memorized or, like the Cuban who called himself Danger, the agonizing dreams they'd had the night before.

Danger said the voices told him to "do this, do this, take a gun, shoot your head." He wanted to be in Cuba again. "I be awake all night long, killing people with guns, knives." But still, he liked to dance the tango. He liked the rock and roll.

Pastor told me never to raise my voice to another patient, Josué, who had become a key member of the staff. "He spent time at San Quentin," Pastor said. When I was there, Josué had been temporarily demoted to the status of patient again because he had used profanity over the staff's CB radio. His punishment was to cut everyone's toenails. Josué was the subject of a documentary being filmed by a British director, Mark Aitken. I'd met Mark at the Judas burning, and I'd see him later in my journey, during a bitter cold snap in late December when five of the patients had died during a two-week period. The much-loved "Crazy Baby" would die in March.

But in May the patients who were not in cells and otherwise physically able were marching or dancing from one end of the courtyard to the other, some like whirling dervishes with their heads thrown back, and Pastor insisted that a thin, childlike man I'll call Angel sing a song. He'd been cutting pineapples for lunch.

"What would you like for him to sing?" Pastor asked me.

I shook my head. I didn't care.

"Just pick one, Angel," Pastor told him in Spanish.

The moment Angel began to sing, I knew I was in the presence of mystery. The lyrics were in Spanish, but the tune was unmistakable. The song was my dead father's favorite, "How Great Thou Art," the spiritual that George Beverly Shea had made famous at Billy Graham rallies in the sixties, including one we'd gone to in Huntsville, Alabama.

Around us, the patients had fallen silent. Some had folded their palms together and lowered their heads in prayer. These were the people—some addicts, some criminals, all afflicted with mental and physical disorders—who'd been rejected even by their own families and left to starve and freeze in the rubble of a city whose citizens were being slaughtered for money and sport.

When Angel finished that first verse and chorus, he turned only to me and sang it all again in English:

> ... *Then sings my soul, My Saviour God, to Thee,*
> *How great Thou art, How great Thou art!*

"Amen!" shouted Pastor as he clapped Angel on the back.

"Amen!" the other patients responded, and they gathered around to hug me and shake my hand.

Afterward I met Petra, a woman in her fifties who'd thrown herself in front of a train because her nephew had broken her piggy bank and stolen ten pesos. She had lost both legs and an arm, but we had a long conversation in the sunlight of the courtyard, and she told me all about her great loves in life: needlepoint and embroidery.

Early this morning, at a bar called Carinosas, they found the body
of a woman who'd bled to death. She was 27 years old, and she'd
been shot 11 times. She was wearing blue jeans, black shoes, and
a white blouse with dark stripes. Beside the body was a blue-green,
school-type backpack with black and white floral prints. She had
a clear, dark complexion, and her hair was long and straight.
　　　　　　　　　 —El Diario, Ciudad Juárez, May 16, 2012

For the rest of the week, the more or less able-bodied men at the asylum
were engaged in a project to salvage medical beds, file cabinets, and
other equipment, including an enormous underground water storage
tank, from a women's AIDS clinic that had been closed because of the
unrelenting violence in its neighborhood. The nonprofit clinic had
donated these items to the asylum, and what Pastor could not use, he
would sell to pay for gas and electricity. Ultimately, he wanted to build a
new wing onto the asylum that would be devoted entirely to the women,
a project only on paper now, but one he was sure he could bring to frui-
tion. The future, for Pastor, was always in the present. As was the past.
On the wall of the AIDS clinic hung a framed poster about the UN's
International Day for the Elimination of Violence Against Women, a
date chosen to honor the four Mirabal sisters—human rights activists
who were murdered in the Dominican Republic in 1960.

Working alongside the male patients in that environment was an
exercise in humility. I was the privileged. They were the deprived.
But they were the ones who never stopped working, who never complained, who never shirked their responsibilities, and who offered
me encouragement all along the way.

We had fun, especially when, after being warned about drive-by
shooters in the neighborhood, we heard the *pop-pop* of small-arms
fire and the clinic began to fill with acrid smoke. I ducked under a
bench and tried to calculate how long I could risk staying there
before being overcome by the smoke. But the other men seemed
undeterred, and when the burly, good-natured staff member I'll call
Pablo pulled out an electric fan, turned it on, and smiled at me, I

saw the hubbub for what it was, a short-circuit in part of the main electrical board. Sparking wires had caused all the popping and smoke.

This was my second misidentification of gunfire in Mexico. The first had been the firecrackers attached to Judas when he burst into flame in the city's main square. It had been thirty years since I'd been a reporter in El Salvador, but loud noises still startled me.

Pastor was in and out of the clinic all day. He kept our spirits up and made sure we had a feast of Mexican street food for lunch and enough money for soft drinks from the corner store and *obleas con cajeta* (crackers with caramel) for dessert. While we were loading trucks after lunch the next day, I looked up just in time to see a man and young woman walking toward us from about a block and a half away. The man, a scrawny, roosterlike figure, suddenly started punching the woman in the stomach. Hard. She bent almost to the ground in pain. I wasn't the only one to see this. Almost everyone else had, too. The woman barely straightened herself enough to stumble into a side street, but the guy just kept walking in our direction—nonchalantly, as though nothing out of the ordinary had happened. He was wearing a short-sleeved green shirt, unbuttoned to show off the tattoos on his chest. This was Juárez, his posture and gait seemed to say. *Chingate.* Fuck you.

Unfortunately for him, Pastor had also seen the whole drama, and he met up with the jerk in the middle of the street. I don't know whether it took one blow or two, but the guy's feet flew out in front of him, and next thing we knew, he was lying on the pavement with Pastor straddling him, fist raised to deliver the coup de grâce. But Pablo grabbed Pastor's arm and held it back in midair. "I'll take it from here," he said, and the two men exchanged places, only Pablo didn't strike the guy, and when the young woman reemerged around the corner from which she'd disappeared and came running up the street to say that the guy hadn't done anything wrong, he was her uncle, he was just playing, don't you see? Pablo let him go.

The guy in the green shirt was cut below his eye and bleeding a little from his nose. He gave us a menacing look, turned without a word, and walked down the street at the same pace as the young woman. But they were not walking close to one another; they were staring straight ahead, and the talk among the patients who had seen the attack was that it was a real and violent one. They said they ought to know.

"Did you see her face?" they were saying. "Did you see the way she looked at us?

"He wasn't her uncle. He was probably her pimp. She was scared of the guy, and now she's scared he's going to take it all out on her."

Somebody suggested we call the police, and everyone else looked startled by the depth of his stupidity. *Don't you know where you are?* those looks seemed to say.

As for Pastor, I had not yet seen him that contrite. He was staring at his knuckles, which were skinned and raw. "I'm so sorry you saw me do that," he said. "I'm ashamed of myself."

"Hey," I said. "You did the right thing. That was a violent attack against a defenseless girl. Everybody saw it. Don't give it a second thought."

"I could have killed him," Pastor said.

I wanted to say, but didn't, that I almost wished he had.

Someone ordered the murder of two women in a bar last night. The first bullet-riddled body was found open-mouthed at the entrance. She was about five feet tall, with dark hair; clear, brown skin; and a robust build. She was dressed in a black blouse, navy blue mesh leggings, and black sandals. The other body was found open-mouthed behind the bar. She was also about five feet tall, obese, and with dark skin. Her hair was red, and she wore a black dress and boots. Police found 16 bullet casings as evidence.

—*El Diario,* Ciudad Juárez, May 18, 2012

On the fifth day, Pastor wanted me to meet a friend of his, an important person in Juárez. He ran a security firm and was a very devout Christian. I'll call him Eduardo. He was a large, athletic man, well dressed in new penny loafers, tan pants, and a yellow golf shirt. He had a warm and engaging smile. We met him at his office, and after a short conversation there, Pastor said he had an errand to run. He hoped we didn't mind going with him and waiting in the car while he shopped at a store or two. He encouraged us to have a good, long conversation. The man's English and my Spanish ought to get us by, Pastor said.

Eduardo was in the backseat, I in the front, and the minute he began his spiel, I suspected he just wanted to save my soul from everlasting hell. His Christian testimony began before we could trade the usual details about our families or where we were from, and I really didn't care for the Road to Salvation as recorded in Paul's letter to the Romans. I'd burned out on that as a teenager, and even in those magical days of spiritual health when my daughters were young, I couldn't bear the rigid, doctrinaire approach to Christianity in that missive. It was like reading a recipe for tuna casserole in one of my mother's old cookbooks.

It didn't take me long to understand that I was hearing something different, something so dark and complex that I started to pay very close attention.

Eduardo said he'd been born in Juárez but became bored in the schools there, so when he reached high school age he moved to the city of Chihuahua, where he played soccer, learned karate, and dreamed of becoming a veterinarian. Instead, he wound up as a police cadet and then as a bodyguard for a corrupt governor of the state of Chihuahua. His cousins cleaned money for Carrillo, the cartel boss in Juárez, and a friend of Eduardo's worked for the Zetas, the superviolent drug gang composed of defected Mexican marines. They had no feelings. It didn't matter to them whether they lived or died.

Eduardo didn't care for drugs, but he was young, and there was money in the illegal drug trade, and many of his other friends were employed by the narco traffickers, so he joined them out of vanity. "The devil," he said, "is very astute." He went to Miami and New York, became one of the zombies. "When you think like an animal, you live like an animal. We lived like animals. Rats love vices."

It was a dangerous game, and Eduardo became addicted to danger. He was hired by the Sinaloa cartel to smuggle hundreds of thousands of dollars' worth of cocaine into Los Angeles, but somebody stole it. Instead of disappearing into America, running away, he returned to the boss of the cartel and explained what had happened. The boss was astonished. He told Eduardo that nobody who had lost a load like that had ever come back to apologize. Until now, they had killed every man they could find who had allowed such a thing to happen. But because Eduardo had come back and stood before the boss and told him the truth, he would be forgiven and could continue to work for them.

His friend with the Zetas, though—they killed him. Fear was a form of control. And ultimately the only thing that could save Eduardo from both vanity and fear was the gospel of Jesus Christ.

"This is a land of lies," he said about Juárez. "The real crime is living here. You have to reclaim your inheritance, your life. Many people believe in God, but not many live as if they do. There's only one way, and that's to be born again, to put off the old man and put on the new."

After Pastor returned to the car, the three of us stopped by the women's AIDS clinic to see how work was progressing. Then we went to dinner at an expensive steak restaurant, the best in Juárez, Pastor said. It was a feast paid for by Eduardo. I thought of the patients while we ate, but decided that Pastor, at least, deserved the extravagance. I sure didn't.

Then, when we drove Eduardo back to his office, he insisted Pastor and I come in long enough for him to play part of a DVD performance by three Spanish tenors. They were extraordinary vocalists, and when Pastor and I said so, Eduardo gave us each a copy of the DVD. "Enjoy it, my friends, and God bless you."

As Pastor drove me back to the asylum, he said, "Eduardo didn't kill anybody."

"What?"

"Eduardo didn't kill anybody," he repeated.

I hadn't said anything to suggest that he had.

A little while later, Pastor said, "If you see a decal for John Deere, it's a car that belongs to the cartel. The Zetas use the John Deere logo here."

"How do you know that?"

"Everybody knows that," he said. "You'd be surprised how much more I know."

Pastor had already told me that hit men had come to the asylum four times demanding the customary *plata o plomo,* silver or lead (a bullet). He had refused the demand each time, as he'd also refused donations from the cartel bosses, no matter how well intentioned. Many of the bosses, he said, were religious, you know, in the sense that they really didn't want to go to hell when they died. So they donated money to build churches and hospitals and convalescent homes for their mothers and wives. But Pastor wasn't ever going to accept money from the devil.

He'd been called in for an appointment with the Juárez prelate because of *La Casa del Diablo,* that painting of his that was the first thing I woke to every morning at the asylum. The prelate thought the piece sacrilegious, whereas Pastor thought the church was cozy with the drug barons and that was the true sacrilege. A taxi driver in the city had once explained it to me this way: "At the bottom," he said, "is us, the amoebas. You can't even see us without a microscope. Then above us are the police. They're like fleas. They can be squished with a finger. And above them are the local politicians, the state governors, and the president and his army. They're like roaches and spiders and rats. And then you get to the church. The church is like the cat that eats the rats, and the cartel bosses, they're the dogs who eat the cat."

The battle lines along the Mexican-American border were not only between the U.S. Border Patrol and the coyotes and drug smugglers, or the Juárez cartel and the one in Sinaloa, but among all levels of Mexican civil and religious society. The religion of death was in constant battle with the religion of life.

At 1:30 this morning a decapitated body with signs of torture was found in an area very difficult to access at the end of Actopan Street where there is no public lighting and low vehicular circulation. The deceased was wearing gray pants, a black belt, and a gray T-shirt. He was found face down and unbound with signs of having been severely beaten before his death. A short distance away, on a rock covered with blood, sat his head, which, it could be noted, was dark complected. The officers said it was possible that he had some tattoos on his back, but this could not be confirmed because the body was so covered with blood. It's not known if a form of identification was found among his clothes.

—El Diario, Ciudad Juárez, May 27, 2012

The next day, we all worked at the clinic, taking leisurely breaks as our fear of drive-by shootings had subsided. Instead of riding back to the asylum on the bus with my fellow lunatics, I let Pastor take me. He wanted to talk again about the beating he'd given to the pimp in front of the women's clinic. "I can't believe I did that," he said. "That's not me anymore."

He told me he had been like that before he'd found the Lord. He'd beaten his wife, picked fights in bars.

I knew he'd been in prison, but I'd never heard that part of the story. When I later asked Chuck if he knew why Pastor had been imprisoned, he said no. I didn't say what Pastor had told me. Perhaps it was an exaggeration. But something was bothering him on the way back to the asylum, that much was certain.

Finally he told me. He said he couldn't get one of the patients to stop smoking. He would confiscate the cigarettes, but the man would always find others. Pastor kept having to put him in a barred and locked cell, over and over and over again. The man pleaded with him, saying, "I can't stop smoking. You know that. I just can't stop!"

Pastor kept telling him the Holy Spirit could help him stop.

"I can't!" the man said.

"But the Holy Spirit can," Pastor said.

Finally, the smoker uttered the words that cut into Pastor's heart. He said, "Yes. But *you're* not the Holy Spirit."

Pastor's voice cracked as he told me this. "He was right," Pastor said, and he actually began to tear up. "I'm not the Holy Spirit. So I let him have his cigarettes. I even bought them for him after that. As long as he smoked outside the walls of the courtyard, I never locked him up again."

That night, I mulled over the conversations I'd had with Pastor in the car and with Eduardo while Pastor was shopping. I couldn't figure out why Pastor had arranged our meeting like that. I knew that Chuck had told him about my journey with the snake handlers of southern Appalachia, and that now I was headed for the Middle East. He'd probably emphasized that I, unlike Chuck himself, was a Christian. So Pastor had welcomed me at the Judas burning as though I were indeed a brother in Christ, but when I told him later that I was searching for faith as a substance rather than a belief, he must have sensed that the search, which I'd tried to frame as philosophical, was personal and as old as Christianity itself.

I'd fallen from grace, and I didn't know how to climb back up. With his ministry in Juárez, Pastor had shown me one of the simple steps: to love the unloved.

If only I could do that.

The next time I saw Chuck and Molly was at a celebration held in a Juárez church for the fiftieth anniversary of Father Peter's ordination as a priest. Afterward we went for a beer at the Kentucky Club, the ornate, wood-paneled, but slightly seedy bar where Marilyn Monroe had celebrated her divorce from Arthur Miller.

"Are you still going to the Middle East?" Chuck asked.

I nodded.

"Well, let me give you a piece of advice." The noise and smoke in the Kentucky Club were unbearable, but if anybody was going to be heard above the din, it would be Chuck Bowden.

"Don't forget to duck," he said.

3

In Love with Things That Vanish

Jesus found our lives here too beautiful, and so invented trials from which only he could save us by his act of continual self-sacrifice. Be that as it may, God's love surpasses all others.

— *My father's message to me in a dream after he died*

A fter stopping to look at the stars in the spring of 2014 on my way to find Kayla Mueller's parents, it occurred to me that if I was really searching for faith in places where people were subject to extremity, maybe I should have started in the place where I'd been a child trying to figure out who I was: Birmingham, Alabama, during the violent days and nights of the American civil rights movement.

My father was a handsome man who liked to dance. We have photos of him in the white linen suit he wore to the Cloud Room behind Cascade Plunge on those Friday nights in the late twenties when all of Birmingham must have been dancing. Mother does not appear in these photographs. Perhaps my father took other girls to the dances. Or perhaps he and his friends went stag. I do know, because he told me, that he and his friends smoked cigarettes in the parking lot when the bands took a break, and sang on the streetcar all the way home.

My sister Jeanie's theory was that Dad would have led a richer, fuller life if only he had married someone who liked to dance. It was useless to point out to her that if that were the case, she and I and our brothers Scotty and Gary would never have been conceived.

Besides, my father had his own reasons for falling in love with Mother. In the cast photo of the high school play in which they met, she is the girl with long blond curls and a flawless but troubling face. Her smile is frank. A childhood in the mining camps does not appear to have broken her spirit. It's true, though, that she did not like to dance, and perhaps that accounted for my own peculiarities. I was born to a man who liked to dance and to a woman who didn't.

I'd find, in time, that the traits my parents shared were what really mattered: personal modesty; selflessness; and a sweet but complicated affection for one another. Their love might not have been perfect, but both of them had faith in a love that was—God's love, which they believed not even the universe was big enough to contain.

For a moment, Dad had hesitated about marriage. One of his friends had wanted him to chuck it all and head for Venezuela after high school graduation.

"They're mining ore in the mountains," his friend told him. "You can get rich if you're quick."

Dad thought the idea crazy. The word "Venezuela," he said to me decades later, sounded like fruit that had gone bad.

But one day, as he and his friend walked past Forest Hill Cemetery, Dad began to give the idea serious thought. He'd just gotten off work stocking shelves after school at Hill's grocery store in Woodlawn, the Birmingham neighborhood where his family of Covingtons lived. It was a late, cold spring, and he said the rain had washed the afternoon so clean, the cemetery headstones looked as though they'd been bleached.

For weeks after that walk by the cemetery, the idea of a new start in a new place wouldn't leave him alone. Especially when his doctor told him he might have the early signs of tuberculosis.

Dad feared he might not live long enough to support and raise a family. He didn't want to be cared for by them as an invalid, or worse yet, in the sanatorium on the hill. If he was going to die anyway, why not die in a far-off paradise? He began to see Birmingham for what it was—narrow-minded and conventional, with houses too small and too much alike, a place where nothing of importance had ever happened and probably never would. What did he have to lose? Who cared if he were to die a zillion miles from where he'd been born? His friend had given him something remote and mysterious to consider. He had said that Venezuela had phosphorescent seas.

In the end, though, the suspicion of TB proved unfounded. The idea of Venezuela disappeared like the dream it was. But after hearing the story for years on end, I would inherit that dream from my father, and in my search for meaning, it would lead me to places where I probably never should have been.

Dad graduated from high school in 1929, at the age of seventeen, and got a job as office boy at Tennessee Coal and Iron. For their first date, he took Mom to see a movie at the Alabama Theatre. A friend had loaned him a car for that. Then he and Mom started going on picnics to Camp Cosby with their other friends, and it was there that Dad proposed to her one day, after which a photo was taken of her sunning on the boat dock, fully clothed.

Mom had not graduated from high school. Her older sister was able to go to college on scholarship and begin a professional career, but their father, Charlie Russell, a loudmouthed railroad detective and strike buster for the coal company, insisted Mom drop out of high school and go to work as a telephone operator. He said they needed the money and she would have to live at home. He added that she was the dumb one, her sister the smart one. That was the kind of man he was, which has led me to believe that Dad might have saved Mom from her father by asking for her hand.

Before they married in 1933, Mom and Dad attended a small, close-knit Methodist church on Georgia Road, where the hymns gave them comfort and hope—hymns like "Blessed Assurance," "Breathe on Me, Breath of God," and "Shall We Gather at the River." The only time members of the congregation spoke during worship was to recite the Apostles' Creed, in which they reaffirmed their belief that God had created the heavens and earth, that his son Jesus Christ had been conceived by the Holy Spirit, born of the Virgin Mary, suffered under Pontius Pilate, and was crucified dead and buried, only to rise again after three days to ascend into heaven, where he sat at the right hand of God the Father Almighty.

John Wesley, the founder of Methodism, had set a modest standard for spiritual ecstasy when he confided, at a place called Aldersgate, that his "heart had been strangely warmed." So the services at West Woodlawn Methodist Church were simple. No one shrieked, spoke in tongues, or was slain in the spirit, all of which I'd later learn so much about. And there were few tears, unless a friend or family member had died, a son had entered the military, or another young person had somehow strayed from the fold.

That was the church in which Mom and Dad were married, and Dad's friend loaned him his car again so Dad could drive his bride downtown for a honeymoon night in the Tutwiler Hotel, the grandest in Birmingham. Neither of my parents had been born to privilege, other than the fact of being white in Birmingham, an enormous advantage that wouldn't begin to be lessened during their lifetimes, or mine, for that matter, at least not by much.

Dad's people had been part of that wave of poor Anglo-Irish immigrants who had come down from the Appalachians after the Civil War to work in the mills and mines of North Alabama. During the Great Depression, he would wind up going to debtors' court. But he would be able to keep his job, and he and Mom never considered themselves poor. They got by, and given the places they had come from and the reversals they would endure, that was more than enough.

I was born in 1948, the youngest of their four children, and I was baptized in another Methodist church, Lake Highlands, which sat on a hill overlooking the Birmingham airport, the city dump, and an all-black neighborhood known as Zion City. Until I was five, we lived in a frame bungalow on the south side of Division Avenue in a neighborhood called East Lake. We had an apple tree and a chinaberry tree in our backyard, and my mother hung the wash out to dry on a line stretched between the two of them. One of my earliest memories is of white sheets billowing in the wind. Another is of hitting the ground when I fell out of that apple tree.

For most of my childhood during the nineteen fifties and early sixties, I knew no world other than Birmingham, and I thought it was the best place and time in which to grow up. I never fretted about having something to eat or wear. I never suffered for lack of medical attention. And I knew that I was loved.

My sister, Jeanie, who was eight years older, treated me as though I were her little prince. My brother Gary, who was twelve years older, wrestled with me on the living room floor until I begged for mercy. And my brother Scotty, fourteen years older and studying engineering at Auburn University, probably saw in me the sons he intended to have when he and his future wife started a family of their own.

Our father was sober and principled. He worked long hours at the steel company during the week and taught the adult Wesley Fellowship Class on Sunday mornings, even rising to chairman of the Board of Stewards for a while. He never spanked or demeaned me. I was his confidant, and he was mine.

My mother would often read a children's poetry book to me before I went to bed, and then she would kneel beside me while we said our prayers. I loved her beyond measure, and would hide behind her skirt when the other children played drop-the-handkerchief after church services on Sunday nights.

In 1954 we moved from the house with the apple and chinaberry trees to one on the north side of Division Avenue, a house with a screened-in front porch and an upstairs bedroom that had been added by the previous owner. Scotty was married by then, and Gary was the one at Auburn, so the upper room would be mine and Gary's when he came home on spring breaks and at Christmas.

I slept in my parents' bed at first, wedged between them for as long as they would let me, which to me was not nearly long enough.

Jeanie's bedroom was at the front of the house, with burglar-barred windows that opened onto the front porch. Sometimes, when Mom and Dad went to church functions, Jeanie would let me fall asleep beside her to the sound of rain on the canvas awning of the porch.

Once I got used to my upper bedroom, I never wanted to leave. I'd crank open the room's jalousie windows and listen to the crickets and frogs, the tree branches creaking in the wind, and the sound of what I imagined to be a wild boar rooting in the wild hydrangea beneath the oak in our backyard. I knew there was no such animal, except as a premonition of something foreign and tragic, a taste perhaps of what it might be like to be an adult. But I was curious instead of afraid. I was open to adventure in the way that most boys are when they know they are safe in their own home.

A year later, one of the neighborhood boys who rode to school with us shot himself in the head while playing Russian roulette with his father's revolver. At his funeral I leaned too far into the casket and accidentally touched my nose to his. I'd been told he was in heaven with God and the angels. But the physical sensation of my nose against a dead boy's never went away.

From the fifth through the eighth grade my classmates and I had the same brilliant young teacher. She would stand in front of the blackboard or perch on the edge of her desk while she told us what she knew about the physical sciences: biology, chemistry, geology, and so forth. When she turned to history, she asked us to imagine how an actual historic event might have occurred and then write a story about it. Mine was the Boston Massacre, in which I imagined boys pelting the British soldiers with snowballs until their elaborate red hats fell to the ground and the soldiers fired their muskets in revenge. She told me I'd done an excellent job. That was when I knew I wanted to be either a writer or a forest ranger.

She also covered the walls of our classroom with maps, which she let us study throughout the day. After my brother Gary came home from the army, I spent an inordinate amount of time studying those maps and wishing I could stay in that classroom and never have to go home.

Later, she urged us to read novels like *To Kill a Mockingbird,* and she gave us individual suggestions as well. For me, she recommended Pasternak's *Doctor Zhivago,* which I read, and re-read, as I lay on the couch in the den at night and tried not to listen to my brother's strange shouts upstairs.

We made scrapbooks about the 1960 presidential election. I played John Kennedy in a class re-enactment of a debate with his chief Democratic rival, Lyndon Johnson. Kennedy's inaugural address stirred something ennobling in me, particularly the last line: "With a good conscience our only sure reward, with history the final judge of our deeds, let us go forth to lead the land we love, asking His blessing and His help, but knowing that here on earth God's work must truly be our own."

Here was a declaration of faith unlike the kind I'd heard in church. It seemed to answer doubts I was starting to have about God's role in the world. Why hadn't he helped the Hungarians when the Russian tanks rolled in, or the Chinese who were dying of hunger? Why had my mother come down with cancer and lost both of her breasts to the disease? I didn't know the details of her surgery at the time: the word "cancer" was only whispered back then, and breasts were not to be mentioned at all. But I knew how serious her condition had been and that she had survived by the grace of God. I also knew, though, that she had suffered before and after the diagnosis, and that even though she was saved by the skill of the surgeons, the cancer might recur. She still might die before her time. If so, would I blame God? After the surgery, she had a "nervous breakdown" and was hospitalized a number of days for that. How did that fit into God's plan for her, or for us?

The world, with all its contradictions, had finally opened up for me. What a challenging and complicated world it was. So was our city; so were our lives. But I was just now beginning to fully grasp how complicated both of them would become.

. . .

Dad had always been honest about the racial violence that surfaced in Birmingham during those years. He was specific when he told me what had happened to black singer Nat King Cole in 1956 as he gave a spring concert to an all-white audience at the Municipal Auditorium. Klansmen had assaulted him—beaten him up, Dad said— and he thought that was a terrible thing for men to do. He was less precise about the Klansmen who picked up a black man near our neighborhood in 1957, took him to a cinder-block shack in the woods and castrated him, pouring turpentine on the open wound before they put him in the trunk of a car and dumped him, barely alive, near Five Mile Creek, where my sister and her friends often went on picnics. Newspaper accounts had used the term "emasculated," and when I asked Dad what that word meant, he said it was the same thing as "mutilated." I accepted his definition, for a while anyway.

All of us knew that my first cousin, Fred Blanton, was an attorney who sometimes represented members of the Klan, but I never told Dad about my Sunday school teacher, who had bragged to us that he himself was a Klan member. I didn't want to get the man in trouble. His daughter was one of my friends, and I knew that Dad hated the Klan because of the terrible reputation its members were giving our city.

When we went downtown on 2nd Avenue North, Dad always pointed out St. Paul's Rectory, where a Catholic priest, James Coyle, had been murdered by a Klansman in 1921. Dad had been nine years old at the time. He would shake his head in utter disbelief that something that horrible could have happened in our hometown.

Most of us think of the Klan as being synonymous with Dixie. But scholars believe that from the end of World War I until midway through World War II, the Klan was stronger in the North and Midwest than it was in the Deep South because its political fear of Jews and Catholics outweighed its hatred of black Americans, who so rarely were allowed to vote in the region.

Many Klansmen and future Klansmen, including Hugo Black,

who would later become a U.S. Supreme Court Justice, thought of themselves as Christian soldiers "going off to war" against the influence of immigrants who threatened their Anglo-Saxon hold on Southern culture, but it was the stories my father told about the Klan that introduced me to the idea that religion could be used for evil as well as good.

It was one thing, Dad said, to be in favor of racially "separate but equal" public facilities, things like schools, restrooms, cafés, even churches. It was another thing to commit violent acts against anyone, for any reason. He had never advocated, or used, violence in his life, he said, and he never would.

But then there was that newspaper photograph from the Birmingham Trailways bus station on Mother's Day 1961, the photo of angular white men in shirtsleeves beating black and white Freedom Riders with iron pipes. I was in the sixth grade at the time, and I was shocked when I recognized, if not the men themselves, then the thing I saw in their faces: the spite and bitter hunger of those poverty-stricken Southern whites who'd come down from the mountains to work in the mills and mines. I suspected even then that I might be one of them.

So when one of Dad's older brothers, Uncle Victor, would visit us from Atlanta and argue that Birmingham's racial intolerance was killing the city's chances of ever becoming a New South metropolis like his, I silently rooted on Uncle Vic's side — but only because he had a dent in his forehead, the result of an automobile accident, and when he sucked jaw breakers as his anger increased, that dent went wild, like a living, breathing animal under his skin.

Dad's side of the argument, that he hated Atlanta traffic, just didn't begin to measure up to that.

But in time I, too, felt the need to defend Birmingham. In the eighth grade, a friend and I, to fulfill one of our teacher's assignments, put together a slide show and taped narrative about the city. We called it "The Birmingham Story." I wrote the script, which we both read. My friend took the slides and chose the music. We pointed out the city's role as one of the world's greatest steel-producing centers, a place where all three of the required raw materials — coal, iron ore, and limestone — could be found in close proximity. Birmingham was also a major railroad hub, we said, from which steel products could be shipped to ports like Mobile for transport to any corner of the world.

Many of the slides were of blast furnaces and steel mills, along with favorite Birmingham tourist sites, including the cast iron statue of Vulcan atop Red Mountain, the Jimmy Morgan Zoo, the Botanical Gardens, the Birmingham Airport, and Legion Field, home of the Alabama-Auburn football game, which was played by white athletes and attended by white spectators. The racial divide in Birmingham was almost as strict as an international border back then.

We included photos of what was considered the nicest "colored part of town," the one with the A.G. Gaston Motel and the Carver Theater and the 16th Street Baptist Church. But there were also photos of the frame shotgun houses that lined the road past the limestone quarries, the dwellings with outhouses in the backyard, chickens in the front, and proud but fatigued black workers trudging home at twilight.

We didn't ignore Birmingham's racial strife. We even quoted from *New York Times* correspondent Harrison Salisbury's famous article about the fear that ruled the city, the article in which he listed the weapons he said had "reinforced the emotional dynamite of racism . . . the whip, the razor, the gun, the bomb, the torch, the club, the knife, the mob . . ."

And we conducted what our local newspaper called "an exclusive interview" with Birmingham mayor Arthur Hanes, in which we asked him when the city's parks and swimming pools might be reopened. They'd been closed because of Birmingham's opposition to racial integration. "How far will Birmingham go to prevent integration?" we asked, and then, "What will the city's action be if an all-out attempt is made to integrate schools?"

I don't remember how the mayor answered those questions, but I do remember that he came to our school to watch our presentation to the class, as did our parents and members of the press.

My friend and I ended on an upbeat note about the goodness of the people of Birmingham, although we had shown relatively few images of its citizens, black or white. Instead, our final slides were of hospitals, churches, and flowering shrubs, and we concluded the voice-over with Proverbs 29:18. "Where there is no vision, the people perish." We followed that verse with a dramatic sunset and the soaring Richard Rodgers orchestral number "Under the Southern Cross" from the TV documentary *Victory at Sea*.

The production was a success. Mayor Hanes said, in an obvious reference to Harrison Salisbury's use of the word "fear" in the *New York Times* article, as well as a nod to Winston Churchill: "The only thing we have to fear is apathy." He added that boys and girls should take an interest in government and that our project had been "a wonderful example."

So my friend and I were minor celebrities among our classmates and families at a time when Dr. Martin Luther King, Jr., was struggling in his plans to turn Birmingham's streets into a world stage for his strategy of nonviolent protest and Police Commissioner Eugene "Bull" Connor was thinking of ways to make Dr. King pay dearly if he tried to do that.

I didn't witness any of those demonstrations downtown in the spring of 1963, except as film footage on the NBC *Huntley-Brinkley Report* on TV, but occasionally I'd hear a distant blast in the night. It could have been a bomb going off at a black church or minister's house on Dynamite Hill, or it just as well might have been an accident at a foundry or railroad yard. But because of those snippets of footage on the national news and the aura of danger in the air, Birmingham seemed to me to be the most important city in the world. I began to argue with my father about what was happening in our city. He had bought into the notion that Dr. King was an "outside agitator." I said that even if he were, that was no excuse to prohibit Negroes from eating at downtown lunch counters or silently protesting in front of the Federal Courthouse. These arguments, although heated, almost always ended amicably. Dad had a way of disarming our disagreements with a comic turn of phrase. But one time I overheard him say to Mom, in reference to me: "Where have we gone wrong?" And as that spring turned into summer and summer into fall, it was clear that Birmingham was headed for a crisis of the kind for which none of us, young or old, black or white, was prepared.

On a Friday night in September of 1963, I was fourteen and sitting on a band bus in Birmingham on the way to one of our high school football games. A girl named Connie Bieker, a pretty clarinetist who would later become a majorette, sat a few rows ahead of me. She had taken off her band uniform coat and was sticking her arm out the window. The night had been hot, and the bus wasn't air conditioned. Up ahead there seemed to be a traffic jam. When the bus slowed to a stop, a black kid not much older than us ran up to the window and slashed Connie's arm with a razor or knife. It was not a serious injury, but I still remember the vivid contrast of blood against the sleeve of her white button-down.

The next morning, as we'd find out many years later, a young woman named Elizabeth Hood stopped by the Birmingham home of her uncle, Robert Chambliss, a Klansman with a history of racial violence and the nickname "Dynamite Bob." Elizabeth told him about the incident on the band bus, the white girl stabbed by a black teenager. She'd read about it in the *Birmingham Post-Herald*. Chambliss flew into a rage. He hurried out to find a copy of the paper, and when he got back, he told his niece to just wait until Sunday morning. He said he had enough "stuff" to flatten half of Birmingham.

And that Sunday, when Mom and Dad and I came home from church, we were joined as usual by my sister, Jeanie; her husband, Bunky; and their two-year-old daughter, Judy. For Sunday dinner, we typically had pot roast, turnip greens, fried corn, rolls, and lemon icebox pie for dessert. My father would keep a pot of coffee going all day long, and later in the afternoon, Bunky and I would go to Krispy Kreme to get a couple of dozen fresh, warm doughnuts to take home.

But we hadn't yet sat down to eat. I don't remember whether Gary was there. If he was, he was up in his room. The details I'm surest about concerning that particular Sunday in September were the ones that had been in my childhood pretty much all along: a metal kitchen table with curved legs and a Formica top, its paramecium design in red and beige; two plaster of Paris bluebirds that clung to the kitchen wall; and a small brown radio on the counter that separated the kitchen table and the stove.

Mother was at the stove when Dad turned the radio on. The rest of us were just standing around, making faces at my niece Judy so we could get her to laugh. That's when we heard the news — a bomb had gone off at the 16th Street Baptist Church downtown and four Negro girls had been killed, three of them my age. The fourth was eleven years old.

I know I must have looked at Jeanie's face first, and she at mine. But after locking eyes with her, I'm sure I followed her gaze toward Dad.

My father was a segregationist, but the finest man I knew. That Sunday morning was the first time I had ever seen him cry, and it was the last time I thought I could ever believe in a merciful and all-powerful God, a god that was both powerful *and* good.

4

The Years the Locust Ate

...baby, we're all running from the same things
Broken hearts, broken homes, the past and the lonely,
loneliness.

— *Amanda Shires, "Ghost Bird"*

I didn't have to go to Vietnam, so later in life, I felt I'd missed my generation's defining, seminal event. Friends who did go to the war told me I was crazy for thinking that. I couldn't help it. I felt guilty. I'd been a drinker and pothead in college, an antiwar activist who had been sitting on a student deferment for four years. But then the draft lottery came along. My number was low. I was drafted; did my basic at Fort Polk, Louisiana; was sent to a leadership preparation course for advanced infantry training; and then, right when I thought I would be headed for Vietnam, was pulled out to be a court reporter on post instead.

I didn't mind Fort Polk. I'd always liked reptiles and amphibians, so Louisiana was fine with me. Sitting through court-martial proceedings and writing them up under the gaze of army lawyers had its ups and downs. I didn't have to record the testimony verbatim, only take accurate notes, so I was able, while sticking to the facts, to make a soldier sound a bit more eloquent than he actually was, just in case the verdict against him came up for appeal.

When there was nothing else to do in the office, I read a book about anti-intellectualism in American life and wrote a couple of poems for our underground newspaper, *The Fort Polk Puke*. At night

I acted in plays by Arthur Miller at the post theater and did volunteer work at the Leesville State School for Retarded Boys. I mainly tried to keep the boys from hurting one another, but I enjoyed their company when there was peace, and I met that disfigured thirteen-year-old whom I never heard speak but who could sing hymns so beautifully it almost resurrected a teenaged dream I'd had of becoming a Methodist minister, one who did mission work among the poor in Appalachia or overseas.

That dream had lasted less than a year. I'd been "saved" at the age of sixteen, but then quickly taken a jaunt to Panama City, Florida, with two of my high school buddies and gotten so drunk I literally could have died of alcohol poisoning that week.

Since I was a trumpeter in the high school band, I played taps at a couple of funerals for Birmingham men who'd been killed in Vietnam, but the deaths didn't seem real to me. I didn't know these guys. They were soldiers, older, smarter. This is what they'd signed up, or been called up, to do. It wasn't until I came home on my first leave from Fort Polk and went to church in my uniform that I realized how blind I had been. After the service I was approached by the parents of Ron Parr, a boy I *did* know—he'd been one year younger than me—and I'd been told he'd died when his tank ran over a Viet Cong mine.

I was uneasy as his parents came down the aisle toward me. Maybe they'd heard I'd demonstrated against the war in college, maybe they knew I was never going to be sent overseas. But when they got to me, and before I could even say how sorry I was about Ron, they each hugged me tightly, more tightly than I'd ever been hugged before, and they told me how proud they were to see me in uniform.

I got married to a young Birmingham woman while I was in the army, and we had a wonderful year in the garage apartment of a Greek family whose mother made moussaka, baklava, almond cookies, and stuffed grape leaves, a woman whose husband, much older than she, gladly drank the Pabst Blue Ribbons I'd gotten for him from the post commissary. It was, my wife and I thought, an even trade.

My wife taught seventh grade in the small town where we lived, and we continued to act in plays at Fort Polk, but because she didn't approve of pot I turned to alcohol again. She was a moderate drinker; I was not. During one of my drunken fits, I told her I didn't want to have a child, because I was afraid she'd try to raise him or her in the church. After the army came graduate school, where I drank considerably more, and then we moved back to Birmingham and the years that the locust ate began.

My wife filed for divorce in 1976. I was teaching in Ohio by that time, and Vicki, another young woman from Birmingham, joined me there. Vicki and I were seasoned, professional drunks by then. But sometime during that year in Ohio, we recognized we had a problem, so we took up bowling instead. It worked for a little while, but not nearly long enough. Vicki hated the Ohio winters. I didn't want her to leave me, so we quit our jobs and moved back to Birmingham, where we "cut back" on our drinking and found work — she as a psychiatric social worker, me as a bus driver and part-time English composition instructor.

By then we wanted to have a child, and one August when we were spending a week in New Orleans, she had a dream. A voice in the dream said, "Look in your mind's eye and see if October fourth falls on a Thursday. If it does, you'll understand what it means."

We forgot about the dream, and upon returning to Birmingham we found out Vicki was pregnant. We hadn't developed the roll of film from New Orleans yet. When we did, one of the photos unnerved us. It had been taken at twilight. She was wearing a bright red dress and standing under a live oak draped in Spanish moss. She looked like a woman who had just seen something dark and unsettling scurry across the road ahead of her.

Two months later Vicki thought she might be miscarrying. The doctor ordered a sonogram and saw no baby in the uterus, so Vicki underwent a D&C. But a few days later, she felt a sharp pain. Her belly seemed distended to her. She lay down, and when I got home from work I was startled by her appearance. Her face was as white as marble. The pain was in one of her shoulders now, she said, and I'd recently read in a pregnancy and birthing book that this might be a sign of internal bleeding somewhere else, so I rushed her to the hospital and she underwent emergency surgery on a Thursday, October 4, the date in her dream. She'd had an ectopic pregnancy. The surgeon took out the Fallopian tube with the fetus in it and tried to salvage the other one, but doctors later told us she had only a ten percent chance of ever conceiving again.

So, as Vicki said in the joint memoir we wrote many years later: "No baby? Then let's wreck the nest."

Which was exactly what we did.

The years that immediately followed were the worst. By the time I got a tenure-track job at the local university, all I wanted to do was escape Birmingham and the kind of marriage ours had become.

I'd been watching the news on TV from El Salvador. There was real suffering there, not the kind we'd manufactured for ourselves. I watched footage of one of the massacres on the steps of the cathedral in San Salvador, the shooting of unarmed students in the back as they lay on their stomachs with their hands behind their heads. Archbishop Romero had been assassinated by then; the four American churchwomen had been raped and killed. But the war had continued, and bodies were being found along city streets and country roads, some propped up naked with their severed heads in their laps. In a nation whose name meant "The Savior," these and all kinds of other ungodly crimes were being committed, but both sides claimed that God was on their side.

The main perpetrators of the slaughter, the death squads and police and army units controlled by the wealthy landowning families, defended their atrocities, arguing that they were saving the country from godless communists. The FMLN guerrillas, on the other hand, excused their lesser but still real bloodletting by invoking liberation theology, which demanded justice for the landless and victimized campesinos, but also resulted in the deaths of Salvadorans whose only crime was standing in line to vote.

I don't think faith had anything to do with what first drew me to El Salvador. Perhaps it was that guilt about not having gone to Vietnam; or a suicidal impulse born of the urge to escape the mess Vicki and I had made of our lives in Birmingham; or simple bloodlust, voyeurism of the worst kind. But whatever the source, I had my ticket in hand, along with a letter from the editor of the *Birmingham Post-Herald* saying that I was on assignment from his newspaper, although I'd never written a word of journalism, never been to a war, never even been outside the United States, and spoke hardly any Spanish except to say, "I'm a journalist. Please don't shoot me." I was on my way to a war, along with a photographer I'd met who had the same fixation, for places where religion bled.

Three distinct moments in El Salvador steered me toward faith. During that first trip, I visited a small town that the FMLN guerrillas had overrun. As many as forty combatants had been killed in the battle and were buried in the streets. Their boots marked the fresh graves. Instead of attempting an escape, some had tried to hole up in the garrison. They'd apparently hid behind bloodied and urine-soaked mattresses at the end.

We could hear the fighting continuing in the fields surrounding the town, but fortunately for us, the mortars were not being walked our way. A few guerrillas were loading supplies from the town store onto the back of an underfed, one-eared horse while we were there, and the children who huddled in the store were as emaciated as the horse, but smiling at me as though nothing would be wrong in their world if only someone could get them out of there. If I'd had the courage, maybe I'd have dared. Courage, though, would take faith, and faith would take courage. The two were intertwined.

I'd been downing margaritas at the hotel bar the night before, but I never drank again in El Salvador after I got back from that town. I stopped drinking entirely a couple of months later back in Birmingham, and then Vicki and I didn't have a single drop of alcohol for seventeen years after that. I don't know what eventually happened to the children in that town, but I do know I owe them for those many years of sobriety.

Another of those moments in El Salvador occurred in December of 1983, when I visited one of the refugee camps outside the city and met three girls who were playing school. One of the girls was the teacher. She was using a piece of gravel to scratch what might have been an arithmetic problem on a sheet-metal wall. The air was as cold as it ever gets in El Salvador. The girls wore no shoes, and there were open sores on their arms and legs. Nobody else in the camp had ventured out of their tents. It was just the three girls until a younger boy ran up to join them.

The tallest of the girls wore a thin blue dress with a white goose stitched on the front. She had a faraway look in her eyes. When I asked about her family, she said her mother had brought her and her brother to the camp after their father's head had been left on their front stoop so that everybody in the village would see it.

This was the week before Christmas. When I got back to Birmingham, I told Vicki about the girl at the camp. On Christmas Eve, we went to church for the first time since we'd been teenagers. A Methodist church in our neighborhood was putting on a Boar's Head and Yule Log Festival, a reimagined celebration from the Middle Ages, with choirs of children and adults and musicians from the Birmingham Symphony Orchestra. There were chimes, bells, and the rattle of drums as costumed participants brought in the boar's head on an enormous platter and rolled in the ancient Yuletide log.

The service was more extravagant than anything I'd ever seen in a church. But the memorable scene for us was the simplest. It happened right before midnight, when the music softened and stopped. Every light in the church dimmed and went out, leaving us in profound darkness. But soon, because Vicki and I were sitting in the balcony, we could see evidence of a wavering light below us. People in the congregation down there were turning around to look. A boy had appeared in the aisle, walking toward the altar. We could just make out the top of his head and the single lighted candle he was carrying before him. He had entered without fanfare or applause, but there was no mistaking who he was. He was the Child who had brought light into the world: "And I will restore to you the years the locust hath eaten..." (Joel 2:25).

After that night, we started attending the church that Vicki had grown up in. We did it surreptitiously at first. We'd come in right before the services started and sit on one of the back pews in our boots, jeans, and flannel shirts. After the Doxology, we'd skip out at the first chord of the organist's recessional and slink off to our childless home.

By the time we found out that Vicki was miraculously pregnant again, we'd joined an adult Sunday school class, and when I headed to El Salvador in September of 1984, she was four months along. Another photographer, a longtime friend, went with me this time, and the third moment of revelation occurred on a trip into the mountains of a rebel-held province, where we had stopped to ask a few questions of the guerrillas standing by the side of the road. The first questions were hardly out of my mouth when the sound of automatic-weapons fire opened up all around us. We'd stumbled into an ambush and had to run for a drainage ditch, where we hunkered down in the mud while the combatants fought it out above our heads.

I knew I was going to die, and as I looked up, I imagined the face of the Salvadoran soldier who would kill me. But what I saw instead was an eye, like that eye in the pyramid on the back of a dollar bill. An enormous eye, steady and clear. Pupil and iris and white, white, white—against which my life rolled out in front of me like a film strip in a seventh-grade science class: scenes that moved slowly through the blue-green iris, the pupil, and the iris again. In the iris, these scenes were as I remembered them but better somehow—the arguments had forgiveness built into them, the tragedies their justice, the deaths their recompense. As the scenes moved into the pupil, though, they became the nightmares of my troubled sleep—the drunken brawls, the blood, the fires, the dead men in the street. But just as suddenly as the images had appeared in the pupil, they entered the iris again, and every wrong had been righted, every trag-edy averted, every infidelity erased, every life and family saved.

I took this vision as a sign that no matter what I'd done in the past, there would be peace and forgiveness in the eye of a benevo-lent and loving God.

Five months after I crawled out of that ditch, our first daughter was born, and two years after that, our second daughter came along, and their births confirmed for us the promise God had made through the prophet Malachi: "...I will...open you the windows of heaven, and pour you out a blessing, that there shall not be room enough to receive it" (3:10).

My last trip to El Salvador during the war was to cover the final guerrilla offensive in the capital in 1989. After peace came to the country, our daughters were old enough to go to El Salvador, too. We'd already taken them, along with other members of our church, on short-term mission trips to South Florida after Hurricane Andrew and to the Belize-Mexico border after disastrous floods had destroyed a town there.

In El Salvador, our team hand-drilled a clean-water well in a remote village where children were dying of diarrhea and intestinal parasites. Our daughters had picked the final spot for the well, and had taken the first turns with the auger. We also went to La Línea, an urban slum on the side of a precipitous ravine down which bodies had been dumped into Lake Ilopango during the war. We did Bible study and arts and crafts with our Salvadoran counterparts. We also worked with them to repair a mission church. Our minister's wife taught smocking—a difficult art as I understand it—to a group of the poorest of the Salvadoran women.

Back home in Alabama, Vicki and I taught Sunday school. She helmed the nursery, and I drove the church bus. The riders I picked up at a halfway home said I looked like Billy Graham. A few of them thought I was. "Morning, Billy!" they'd say when they boarded the bus, and "God bless you, Billy!" they'd say when I let them off.

Our daughters tutored preschoolers in an inner-city school, and all four of us were members of our church's AIDS Care Team. I remember singing to one of the patients as he lay dying. He was a black drag queen, a young man my daughters dearly loved. He had wanted me to sing "Turn Your Eyes Upon Jesus" as he breathed his last. To be asked by him was a gift.

Does it take going to a war to find meaning, to find faith? To find something beyond religion, beyond belief? I can't speak for anyone else. I can only speak for myself. The racial hatred in Birmingham had caused me to abandon my faith. The suffering during the war in El Salvador had restored it to me.

The trouble with faith, though, is that it's not stationary. This idea that you set your compass by it, and then your life's nothing but smooth sailing forevermore—is baloney. From what I know about the lives of saints, faith is not even like that for them, and for me, it's been like the dial on an old car radio. Turn that dial too far one way or the other and you lose reception. Turn it way too far, and the mechanism breaks. You're lost again. You might never get the music back. So there are no easy answers and no easy ways to find and receive "the substance of things hoped for." There's risk involved, as there was when I hung out with the snake handlers of southern Appalachia in the early nineties and experienced the power of the Holy Spirit.

Faith is a gamble, like life itself, and after Vicki and I gambled everything in late middle age when we fell in love with other people, I had cancer surgery, suffered severe depression, went bankrupt, and moved a thousand miles away. We would eventually divorce. Our younger daughter joined me in that abandoned farmhouse on the edge of a canyon fifty miles from the university where I taught. Our older daughter joined the Marines.

The years the locust ate had returned to haunt me. The abandoned farmhouse was missing half a crucial wall, so rattlesnakes and scorpions got into the living room, where my dog and I slept together on the floor. My daughter and I scavenged wood and from the dump a rusted-out barbecue grill and skillet to fry eggs on, and the pipe that ran from our toilet ended in a cesspool out back. When it got blocked, I'd have to dig a trench, saw the pipe, reach in to pull out the blockage, and then reseal the sawed ends. Nothing a plumber couldn't do in a jiffy, if only there had been one, and if only I could have paid him or her. Same for the pipes from the well that froze every winter. Then there were the wild boars that showed up at night during lightning storms to terrify the crap out of us when we walked outside.

We did, however, have friends there, our nearest neighbor and his wife. They were ranchers, the very finest Christians I think I've ever known. Their house was about a mile away from us, one of only three visible as far as the horizon, and that horizon was very, very far away. They told us this part of Texas was literally the flattest place on earth, "so flat," they said, "that you can see your dog run away for three days." They gave us a stove and brought vegetables from their garden and fruit from their trees. They repaired that wall and replaced our well pump and taught us how to be as self-sufficient as we could be.

What we experienced during that time was nothing, absolutely nothing, compared to what the people in parts of northern Syria would be going through a decade later. Clean water, sufficient food, medical care, security? These were impossibilities there, where children were being raped to death and families burned alive while Americans, in particular, just didn't seem to care. Nobody got it when I shared the fact that Aleppo was known for two things: the best soap in the world and the "River of Death," into which hundreds of civilians had been thrown after being executed on the spot. When I reminded acquaintances that Americans who went over there to help were among the Westerners who were being kidnapped and tortured, they stared at me as if I'd gotten out the wrong side of the bed that morning.

Did I want to go so I could do some good over there? No, I just wanted to go so I could write about faith as an action rather than just a set of beliefs. I don't think even my Syrian friends understood, any more than I did, what I meant by that. But I had accepted the suggestion in Hebrews 11 that belief and faith might be two separate things.

I had not been able to find a church in Texas and had resorted instead to a kind of primitive religiosity in which I placed my faith on chance. The roll of the dice, the results of the draw. The closest church to the abandoned farmhouse, for instance, had been Pentecostal and nine miles away. The congregation was almost entirely Hispanic, and the pastor was postmaster of the county seat, which had fewer than 1,900 inhabitants.

Attending that church was good for my Spanish and good for my sense of self-worth in the eyes of a God that I still longed to serve in some way. But one Sunday, when the young people in the church were on retreat in another part of the state, the pastor gave a sermon that was political in nature, the only spiritual component being the announcement that our president was the Antichrist. I couldn't go back after that. For all I knew, the president might have been the Antichrist, but the announcement of it as a certainty in the church I attended was one of those things I just couldn't abide. I missed the music, preaching, and goodwill of that church, and I despaired of finding anything to take its place. My graduate students at the university, the ones with families, tried to get me interested in their churches, but I always felt like damaged goods whenever I walked through a church door with them. If there was a God, I couldn't possibly be worth anything to the him or her that slept in those fine places.

I'd turned into a prisoner of the past. I wanted that state of grace I'd felt when I would come back to Birmingham after a visit to El Salvador during the war, or the one our family experienced when we were doing simple service for others but receiving much more from them in return.

So in 2012, I had jumped at Chuck Bowden's invitation to join him in Juárez. He knew something I didn't know. He was not a believer, but he was a far better man than I, and he recognized that Pastor's asylum in the desert was a tangible manifestation of what I said I was looking for. I could have stopped there in Juárez and devoted myself, as Pastor did, to loving the unloved. But I didn't know then what I know now, that I'd found something powerful at the asylum, something worth staying for. Instead I went to the Middle East, to Antioch in particular, at the beginning of what would become the worst religious war, and greatest humanitarian tragedy, of our time.

5

What I Didn't Tell the Woman
from Kyrgyzstan

On the flight from JFK to Istanbul, a woman from Kyrgyzstan told me she had a solution for the conflict in Afghanistan. "Just send them gay boys and lots of ecstasy. They'll forget about fighting then." This woman was thin, fair-skinned, and clothed in natural fibers and sturdy footwear. She said she was a self-employed liaison between American donor groups and worthwhile aid projects in Afghani villages. "They like gay boys," she whispered.

"I understood you the first time," I said. "Your English is better than mine."

"I have a master's degree in international relations from one of your major universities," she said, "and I'm also fluent in Dari, Farsi, and Russian."

This stopped me. "Who did you say you worked for?"

"Do you really expect an answer to that?"

I didn't, so I told her my own story instead: that I was from Alabama by way of Texas and that I had just put my brother into a nursing home, even though I questioned whether he wanted to be there. I was on my way to the site of ancient Antioch, where Christians had first been called Christians and where Saint Paul had begun his mission trips to the Western world. I told her I was looking for faith.

The woman from Kyrgyzstan shrugged. "I don't have any use for religion," she said. "The men I work with are addicted to pornography, but they don't approve of the way I dress."

It was midafternoon in Istanbul when we landed. As we collected our bags from the overhead bin, I thought the woman from Kyrgyzstan might wish me a safe trip, but she was already halfway to the exit before she turned and said, "If you're really looking for faith, maybe you ought to just take care of your brother."

What I wished I had told the woman from Kyrgyzstan was that when my brother Gary came home from the army in the summer of 1959, he and I were expected to share a bedroom at the top of the stairs. It was pine-paneled and spare, with twin beds, a nightstand, and a closet where he had stored his .22 and shotgun while he'd been away. At night I'd lie in bed and listen to the crickets, the wind through trees, or the roar of an engine on the test stand at Hayes Aircraft, where our married older brother, Scotty, worked. Then I'd read Hardy Boys mysteries until Dad called up to tell me it was time to turn off the gooseneck lamp and go to sleep.

Mom and Dad always said that Gary had been a quiet, polite boy. Won a baby beauty contest when he was two. Made good grades in school, never caused any trouble. When I was five, he took me on the streetcar to see my first movie, *The Creature from the Black Lagoon,* and later I imagined that he and Pudgy Pledger, a motorcycle-riding friend of his, had stepped right out of *Rebel Without a Cause.*

But after high school and a couple of years at Auburn, Gary enlisted in the army and became a radio operator in a motorized communications outfit at Fort Sam Houston in San Antonio. He drove a jeep with a huge transmitter in the back, and spent a lot of time on maneuvers in the desert. Toward the end, he and the rest of his unit were prepped to go to Beirut, but the Pentagon wound up sending the Marines instead.

Gary hadn't cared much for the army, but he'd liked San Antonio as an exotic idea. One day, when he was home on leave, he said he'd seen two men quarreling on a front porch in San Antonio. They were shouting at each other in Spanish, and Gary didn't understand a word, but he remembered how they'd fought with their fists and then with anything close at hand. One of them broke a chair over the other man's head, and Gary recounted that scene with a light in his eyes. "I wonder if they're still at it," he said as we play-boxed in the downstairs den under the plastic longhorn steer horns he'd brought me from San Antonio.

Gary completed his full term of service with an honorable discharge, and after he came home from the army for good, things took a turn. He was twenty-two, and I was ten. In the upper bedroom we shared, I never saw him read or sleep. He'd leave the bedside lamp on all night and chain-smoke Parliament cigarettes, the kind with the filters recessed a quarter inch. When the ashtray was full, he'd flick ashes on the floor, or just lay the cigarette on the nightstand and let it burn its way out. Then he'd put his forearm to his mouth and chew on it until the skin broke and there was blood, and later scabs. He'd also make strange noises, animal sounds and muttered obscenities, and one night his voice was loud enough to wake Dad.

This was 1959. My nuclear family didn't know much about mental illness. We knew what syphilis had done to Grandfather Russell's brain, and we knew that my father's oldest sister, Aunt Mary, had died of cancer in the state mental hospital. But all we knew about Gary when he came home from the army was that something terrible was happening, both to him and to us.

Dad told me to bring my stuff down to the den, where he'd made a bed for me on the sofa. He said it would be best if I slept there until my sister got married in September. Then I could have her bedroom at the front of the house, far away from whatever it was that was going on upstairs.

For the rest of that summer I'd wake in the middle of the night to the creak of the upstairs floorboards followed by the low, familiar whine and the gasping sounds Gary made when he inhaled and cursed at the same time. I knew he'd have his forearm in his mouth, worrying the raw skin near the wrist, tossing his head, blinking and rolling his eyes. Then the ceiling above me would shake. I'd hear a "*Gott...*" followed by gibberish at the top of the vocal scale, the kind of racket small mammals make when cornered, then "*Got*damnmother-fucking sonofabitchgod*damn*," followed by more gibberish. A *whomp,* this time against the wall perhaps. Low, threatening interrogation. Short squeals, another *whomp.* "Gotdamn motherfucking godfucking bitch ah ah goddamn oh motherfuckingsonofabitch got*damn*..."

Dad passed through the den on his way to the stairs. I noticed how he took them one at a time, deliberate in the darkness. "Jesus-fucking *got*damn sonofabitch..." And I knew that by the time Dad had reached the top of the stairs, Gary would have fallen silent, slipped between the sheets, and rolled over on his side. He knew about, and could control, his outbursts that much, at least.

Dad had probably said, "Son? What's wrong, son?"

And I could hear my brother's remarkable reply as it drifted down the stairwell: "What? Oh, nothing."

That was what the nights were like in that house in Birmingham after Gary came home from the army. In the mornings, after Dad had left for work and Mom was cooking breakfast for us, Gary would pace in a semicircle behind her, chewing his arm, growling and curs-ing under his breath, and stopping only long enough to sing a song he'd made up, a song like "The N-double-A-C-P...is after, after me!" or (to the tune of "Camptown Races"): "I'm gonna rob a big old bank...doo dah...doo dah."

No friends ever visited us that year or the next, except for Pat and Molly Stevens, and then only when Gary was upstairs and I had the TV in the den turned up loud. The adults would drink coffee, Dad and Pat would smoke cigarettes, and all four of the adults would laugh at the jokes Pat told, most from his work at the post office, and at moments like those it was almost as though we lived in an ordinary house in an ordinary life, except for the background noise upstairs that not even the loudest variety show or comedy hour could drown out.

In the meantime, Gary wouldn't even acknowledge that he was doing anything odd, let alone agree to see a doctor about it. He was over twenty-one. Mom and Dad couldn't force him to. In desperation, Dad finally filed a police incident report, which resulted in a charge of disturbing the peace and a night in a Birmingham jail. The only peace that had been disturbed was our own, but Dad said this had to be done so that Gary could be seen by a physician.

On the Saturday that Dad was to drive Gary to Hillcrest, a private hospital in Birmingham that specialized in treating patients with mental disorders, he asked Ralph Vaught, a friend from his Sunday School class and a member of the Civil Defense, to be there to help reason with Gary, and to provide backup if Gary didn't cooperate. Dad told me to take a walk to the lake at the city park a few blocks away, where I often spent my afternoons hunting for baby turtles or the snakes that hung from the branches of trees along nearby Village Creek, an open sewer that wound, like a rivulet of disease, through the black and white neighborhoods of Birmingham. It would be best if I weren't there, Dad said, best for me, and also best for Gary. At the lake I often dreamed I was Tom Sawyer or Huck Finn, with nothing but the open water ahead of me. Sometimes I stood or sat like that for an hour or more, no longer even pretending to be hunting for turtles. But this time, curiosity got the best of me after twenty minutes or so. I didn't want to go back to the house, but something told me I would regret it later in life if I didn't, so I walked halfway back down the alley from the lake and saw that both Dad's car and Mr. Vaught's car were still in the driveway.

There was a low, detached section of roof above the steps that led to the outside door to the basement. From it, one could see the kitchen, the kitchen table, and the island that separated them. I climbed up on that roof, stayed as low as I could, and peered over the windowsill. Dad, Mr. Vaught, and Gary were seated at the table. The older men were smoking cigarettes, their coffee cups shoved off to one side. Gary was facing me, but his eyes were looking straight down at the table. He was wearing his tan windbreaker, his hands stuffed into its pockets. I was afraid he'd look up, so I pressed my cheek down on the hot asphalt tile of the roofing and tried not to move a muscle. I stayed like that until I heard a chair scrape back, then a second, then a third. When I looked up, Gary was headed, in no particular hurry, toward the back door. Dad caught up with him at the sink. He reached out for Gary's arm, tenderly, it seemed to me, but Gary jerked back at the touch, and his elbow flew up and collided with Dad's mouth, sending his false teeth clattering into the sink.

I'm sure Gary didn't intend to do that. But what was done was done. He backed toward the door, turned to slowly open it, and walked out with the resolute step of someone who has nowhere to go but is nonetheless intent on losing himself there.

I was terrified he'd come around the corner of the house and see me, a crouched witness to his humiliation, but there was nothing but silence for the longest time, until I heard the engines of the cars start one after the other, heard their sounds fade into the distance, and understood that Gary had given in. He would be in the lead car, with Dad at the wheel. Mr. Vaught would be behind, in case there were further problems on the way to what Gary would hereafter call "the loony bin."

Not long after being admitted there, he escaped and thumbed north to Decatur, Alabama, where Scotty was now working as a test-stand engineer at the Marshall Space Flight Center in nearby Huntsville. Scotty and his wife had a two-year-old son and another on the way. I don't know what made Gary think they would give him sanctuary. Instead, Scotty called Dad, Dad called the police, and Gary was returned to a hospital, but this time Bryce State Mental Hospital in Tuscaloosa, to which Dad had committed him. Gary, of course, never forgave Scotty for that.

The doctors at the private hospital in Birmingham had administered electroshock therapy, but the ones at the hospital in Tuscaloosa didn't go that far. They put Gary on antipsychotic medication and assigned him to occupational therapy, which consisted of filing patient records in the state mental hospital's office, before they transferred him to the VA hospital across the highway. He unloaded trucks at the facility's warehouse until he just walked away from there for good.

He had slipped under the radar and rented an apartment in Tusca-loosa, where he began working at a thrift store. The job didn't last long, though, so he caught a bus back to Birmingham, and our parents took him in. I was twelve, and the arm-gnawing, cursing, and banging against walls continued for as long as I lived in that house. There was often something funny about it, like when he'd march around reenacting scenes in which he'd use different voices to threaten, cajole, or plead with people we couldn't see, but Mom and Dad began locking their bed-room doors at night, because between the strings of obscenities my brother would often threaten to kill them in that high-pitched, disem-bodied voice he'd first used when he was lying in the twin bed next to mine. Only once, when I was a teenager, did I hear that threat directed at me. I can't recall the exact words, but the gist was clear—that after he'd done it, he'd have to stuff me in a bag and dispose of it somewhere.

I was old enough by then to shrug off what he'd said. But I couldn't understand why he continued to deny that anything was wrong and why he refused to take his antipsychotic medication. To compensate, Mom would doctor his instant coffee with it. "No, no, don't use that jar," she'd say. "That's his."

Other than that incident at the kitchen sink, I never saw Gary hurt Mom or Dad physically, but one night my sister, Jeanie, thought she had. She'd stopped by the house to retrieve a diaper bag when what she saw through the glass in the back door took her breath away. A chair was raised above Gary's head, and he began to bring it down again and again as if to finish off an unseen enemy who was lying on the floor. Jeanie punched her fist through the glass so she could unlock the door from the inside, but when she opened it, she saw there was nothing on the floor but the remains of the broken chair. She didn't look into Gary's face. She just turned and ran down the back stairs, got into the driver's seat of her white Ford Falcon, and pressed her bleeding hand to her heart until she could get home to bandage it.

"You're the only one he trusts," Mom and Dad always told me. "Just keep pretending that you don't notice what happens when he gets...you know, that way."

So that's what I did. I pretended that nothing was amiss. My brother Gary and I never shared a cross word. When we talked, it was always about the military, animals, or Auburn football. He liked to play golf and I didn't, but he persuaded me to at least lift weights with him at the downtown YMCA, and in the car on the way home, we'd reminisce about the years before he came back from San Antonio. I continued to pretend that nothing unusual had ever happened, even after I got married in 1971 and nearly drank myself to death, and after my second wife and I sobered up in 1983, had our kids, and returned to church. I pretended after that second marriage took a bad turn in the late nineties, and after I went bankrupt and accepted a new job offer in Texas, the state where I'm sitting right now. I pretended until everyone in my nuclear family—Mom and Dad, Scotty and Jeanie—was dead. Everyone, that is, except the brother who'd screamed obscenities, chewed his forearm, and pounded the walls. Everyone except him and me. I pretended for more than fifty years. I pretended until the spring before I boarded that plane from JFK to Istanbul and the woman from Kyrgyzstan told me if I was really looking for faith, maybe I ought to just take care of my brother.

6

All We Have Is God

Behold the fowls of the air: for they sow not, neither do
they reap, nor gather into barns; yet your heavenly Father
feedeth them. Are ye not much better than they?
— *Matthew 6:26*

In July of 2012, on my first visit to the Turkish-Syrian border
region, some fishermen told my translator, Henri, that they'd
heard explosions and seen a Syrian army tank and helicopter firing
on refugees who were trying to flee into Turkey near a village called
Güveççi. A Syrian army general had been among the fleeing refugees.

At the time Henri and I were headed to Yayladağı, a border town
about a forty-minute drive from Antioch, but after encountering the
fishermen, we turned off the highway onto a rutted dirt road that
ran under the shade of almond trees and through an occasional herd
of goats, toward Güveççi. Along the way, Henri slowed to wave at a
man who was swatting his donkey's flank and at another who'd been
fishing from a reservoir just outside of town and was holding aloft
his catch, a monstrous carp.

The town of Güveççi clung to the side of a mountain near a Turkish army fort that commanded a view of the broad valley below. On
the floor of the valley, between strands of barbed wire overlooked by
green observation towers, Turkey and Syria met in the middle of a
rivulet that would become the Orontes before it sliced through
Antioch on its way to the sea.

The village on the Syrian side of the border appeared deserted.

A multistory building on the hill behind it looked as though it had been pulverized by artillery fire.

Henri parked the car and told me to follow him down a narrow alley to the patio of a house that offered what must have been the same panoramic view as that of the Turkish fort. He said he'd been to this place before. The patio was occupied by six men in fatigue pants, T-shirts, and athletic shoes. They were sitting on wooden chairs pulled into a rough semicircle, and they stopped talking the moment they saw us approach. None of them appeared armed, but when Henri introduced us, they glanced sideways at one another as though they were unsure whether they were allowed to talk.

Henri explained that I was an American and that we just had a few questions. We'd heard that Syrian regime helicopters and a tank had come down the valley pursuing refugees.

One by one, the men concurred. They said the tank had passed within fifty meters of where they'd been standing. Then they looked at one another again, as though to confirm that it was all right to continue.

"Bashar has tanks, bombs, and helicopters," one of them finally said, "but we don't even have guns." He stopped, looked at his hands, and then raised them, palms up. "All we have is God." It must have been something from the Quran, I thought.

The youngest rebel, a teenager with a pale birthmark running from forehead to cheek, quickly added that America had the power to help them. He looked straight at me. "You helped Iraq. Why don't you help us?"

I asked the boy, through Henri, how long he'd been fighting.

The boy said he had served in the Syrian army, as all males were required to do, but that he had quickly deserted and joined the rebels.

Henri asked him why he didn't just try to find work in Turkey, start a family, a new life.

The boy looked offended. "I was born in Syria," he said. "I will die for Syria."

Our talk ended when a much older rebel with an automatic pistol appeared on the patio and motioned for the fighters to shut up and for us to scram, which we did, stopping only for crackers and Cokes at a corner store before heading to Yayladağı, the much larger border town to which we'd originally been headed.

I'd been able to visit Antioch because my university had awarded me a travel grant to deliver a scholarly paper at an international ethics conference on the island of Cyprus. I was a professor of creative writing, which had very little to do with either scholarship or ethics, but I wrote and delivered the paper anyway. Then I took a ferry to the Turkish mainland.

The uprising in Syria was what had interested me, and the Turkish town of Yayladağı was the location of the official border crossing, then closed, that led to the northwestern Syrian city of Latakia, Syrian president Bashar al-Assad's ancestral home and the site of one of his palaces. Many thought it would be the place to which he would retreat for his last stand, if it came to that. Yayladağı was also a haven for members of the rebel Free Syrian Army and for the ordinary Syrians who'd been trying to escape the fighting, refugees like the ones who'd been pursued by the helicopters and tank as they crossed into the town of Güveççi.

When Henri and I pulled up in front of the refugee camp in Yayladağı and got out of the car, we were approached by three figures who had been standing in the shade of an avocado tree. One was gray-haired and wearing dark slacks. The second was burly and heavily bearded. He loudly identified himself as a Free Syrian Army commander. The third was a cute, skinny boy in fatigues. He was limping, and he winced as he tried to keep up with the other two.

The rebel commander asked Henri if we could give the three of them a ride to Harbiye, a town that adjoined Antioch. Harbiye was the legendary site of the pool where the virgin Daphne had been turned into a laurel tree and her lovestruck pursuer, Apollo, had no alternative but to sit in her shade, plucking and smelling her leaves one by one.

Henri shrugged off the request. He told the man that we'd just come from Antioch and that we wanted to talk to refugees at the camp here in Yayladağı.

"Why not talk to us?" the commander said. He leaned closer. "This brother beside me is a Syrian army general who has defected to our side. What do you say?"

Henri glanced at me. *A Syrian army general?*

"Sure," I said, and the three climbed into the backseat.

"What's wrong with the boy in back?" I asked Henri as he pulled away from the curb, and he passed the question along to the rebel commander.

"What's wrong with him?" the commander said. "I shot him."

"Why?" I asked.

"Because he's a Syrian soldier."

I found that hard to believe. The boy looked no older than fifteen, but when I insisted that Henri ask the boy himself, he confirmed that he was seventeen, that he was indeed a Syrian soldier, and that his name was Muhammed.

"Yes, I shot him," the commander repeated. "Then I brought him to the refugee camp. They bandaged him up, and now we're taking him back to his family in Syria."

He said the three of them intended to catch a bus from Harbiye to Reyhanlı, another border town, but one at which the border was open and where he knew the guards. They'd have a better chance there of crossing safely back into Syria.

When Henri asked about religion, the rebel commander said he was Sunni, as was the gray-haired Syrian army general. The seventeen-year-old soldier he'd shot, though, was Alawite, the same Islamic sect as that of Bashar al-Assad. The commander said he hadn't shot the boy because he was Alawite. He'd shot him because this was a war. Religion had nothing to do with it.

"What has America been thinking?" he said. "Everybody in Syria, no matter what their beliefs, used to live together in peace. But now all of us just want to get rid of Bashar al-Assad!"

Bashar's father, Hafez al-Assad, had staked his dynasty in Syria on the creation of what appeared on the surface to be a secular state, but using the Sunni/Alawite distinction to his advantage when it was convenient to preserve his dictatorship. He'd revealed his true colors in 1982 when, in response to a revolt by members of the Muslim Brotherhood, he massacred as many as twenty thousand Sunnis in the town of Hama.

After Hafez al-Assad's death in 2000, his son Bashar became president. Bashar was an ophthalmologist and had taken the reins of power only because his older brother had been killed in an automobile accident. While Bashar claimed to be inclusive and secular in his outlook, when demonstrators from all religions took to the streets shouting "We are One!" during the Arab Spring of 2011, Bashar tried to pit the minority Alawites against the majority Sunnis.

So the rebel commander was probably right in saying that Syrians of different beliefs had lived together in peace, but only as long as Bashar's dictatorship remained unchallenged. The moment it was, Bashar unleashed his secret police, the Mukhabarat, and ultimately his entire armed forces.

I glanced back at the former Syrian army general, hoping he would join the conversation, but he remained silent and simply stared out the window at the refugees lined up on the sidewalk for bread. Finally he turned and said, "Both Russia and America want to kill these people. Nobody's on our side. All we have is God."

That was the second time in one day that I'd heard those words. I couldn't decide whether the general was just using the phrase to emphasize his disgust with American policy toward Syria, or whether it was a statement of genuine religious belief. If it was an article of faith, did he mean that God was enough, that he was sufficient for all our needs? Or did he mean that God was the last resort, the only thing left?

The rebel commander's interpretation was clearly political: "Bashar is a dictator. He's tortured and murdered thousands of people, even children. Your president said that Bashar has to go, but he hasn't done anything to help us get rid of him!"

He and Henri wound up talking all the way to Harbiye, but Henri rarely took time to translate, unless the commander had aimed a particularly sharp barb at Americans, or Westerners in general, for their refusal to provide military aid to the Free Syrian Army. Sometimes Henri would laugh along with the commander, sometimes not.

I didn't know Henri's politics yet, and his expressions betrayed neither solidarity nor disapproval. As I'd find out later, his face hardly ever registered more than one of two emotions at any time: either glee when he'd made a sly joke at the expense of someone else, or rage when he'd jump out of the car to pick a fight with the guy who hadn't yielded to him in a roundabout. I actually came to like that very thing about Henri—his predictability—except when he hunkered over the steering wheel, pressed the pedal to the floor, and shouted, "I'm Formula One!" He'd be ticketed for speeding three times while I was with him, and during a torturous descent from the mountain town of Kilis in January, I'd have to ask him to pull off into a snowbank so I could throw up.

I also found out that Henri was Christian, and Turkish by birth but fluent in Arabic because his mother and father had originally come from Aleppo, Syria's largest city and commercial hub. Aleppo was only forty kilometers or so from the Turkish border, but it was already the scene of fierce street fighting between the Free Syrian Army and the regime forces of Bashar al-Assad. Many members of Henri's extended family still lived in the city, and his wife also had family there.

When Henri and I let our passengers off at a bus stop on a busy street corner in Harbiye, the gray-haired general who had defected to the rebel side was smiling and thanked us for the lift. The bearded rebel commander, still brooding, also thanked us. But the seventeen-year-old Syrian army soldier never raised his eyes as the rebel commander helped him out of the car. When he slowly straightened up and saw the traffic whizzing by, he looked as though he didn't really believe that he was still alive.

I couldn't help but wonder whether the rebel commander's story was true, and whether the boy might not have been brought into

Harbiye for reasons other than eventually being returned to his family in Syria. The story didn't quite add up.

"So what were you and the commander talking about all that time?" I asked Henri.

"The situation in Syria," he said.

"What'd he say?"

"He said it was bad."

"That's it? Bad?"

"Very bad," Henri said. "Hey, would you like a cigarette?"

I shook my head. Henri was either the most cautious translator I'd ever used, or the least forthcoming.

"You don't smoke?" he said. "What's the matter? Are you Muslim?" He grinned, as I knew he would.

That afternoon we ate lunch at an outdoor restaurant with tables set up in the middle of the stream that ran from Daphne's falls into her pool. We ate barefooted and let the water rush across our feet. It reminded me of a verse from the Gospel of John: "If I then, your Lord and Master, have washed your feet; ye also ought to wash one another's feet." (13:14)

We used to do that in the Sunday school class I'd taught many years before. The students were teenagers and loved foot washing's radical nature. It was a secret between us. When the church deacons got word about what we were doing, they were horrified, or so I was told.

I thought, too, of Pastor, the way he served his otherwise abandoned flock in Mexico, and the way they cared for one another's needs, literally washing the ones who were incontinent or otherwise physically unable to bathe themselves. I thought of "Crazy Baby," the murderer who brushed everyone's teeth, and of Josué, the patient who, when he was briefly relieved of his staff duties for using profanity on the radio, was delegated the task of cutting everyone's toenails. The door of the asylum's courtyard was always unlocked. Unless you were temporarily in a barred cell because you'd hurt one of the other patients, you were free to leave the asylum and go out into the world whenever you wished. To stay and serve — that was a kind of freedom I'd never considered before.

I had a couple of days to kill in Antioch, the City of Peace. I took a long walk along the Orontes River, through a park with palm trees, fountains, geese, and cafés where men played backgammon and boys played electronic games on their iPhones. I walked back over a lovely white bridge where traditional Muslim couples rendezvoused, yards apart and with little eye contact between them. My hotel, the Liwan, was located on a modest strip of restaurants and boutiques that were packed with teenage girls in jeans and T-shirts, often with provocative slogans in English. Some of the girls wore head scarves but almost all the adult women wore them, and the most conservative women wore black abayas and even veils.

The vast majority of Antioch residents identified themselves as Muslim. Most were Alevi — a mystical, particularly Turkish branch of Shi'a that resembled Syrian president Bashar al-Assad's minority Alawite clan. This was no wonder, since Antioch and its province, Hatay, had belonged to Syria until 1939. In an attempt to enlist Turkey's support during World War II, the Allies had offered President Mustafa Kemal Ataturk that piece of northwestern Syria containing Antioch, which was rich in archaeological and religious significance. Ataturk gladly took the land, but reneged on his pledge to commit Turkey to the Allied cause. Turkey remained neutral during World War II, and the land that had been gifted to it, land that hung like a pendulum into Syria proper and was peopled predominantly by Syrian Alawites, would become an ongoing source of friction between Turkey and Syria and a potential flashpoint in what has threatened at times to morph into a Turkish/Syrian war.

In Turkey as a whole, Alevis were so small a presence they were not even recognized as members of an organized religion. But in Antioch, the situation was reversed. The minority in Antioch were Sunni, the predominant form of Islam in Turkey and the rest of the Muslim world. And although at the time of this writing Alevis are still a majority in Antioch, Sunnis are increasing rapidly in number as refugees from northern Syria flood into the city.

Christians, in this city where Christians were first called Christians, now account for only about two percent of the population; I have been told that the number of elderly Jews is in the single digits.

But for all that Islamic predominance, and the tension within it, there is still a deep-seated pride in Antioch's history as an important and holy site for all three major monotheistic religions. To watch this pride turn to fear may be a consequence of the war at Antioch's doorstep, or it might be the historic animosity between Sunni and Shi'a that has festered beneath the surface of Islam for centuries.

A German tourist I met at the Liwan was Sunni. He preferred not to give his name. He was on vacation, although he hadn't brought along his wife and kids. To the question *Why here?* he said because it was too cold in Germany. *In July?* He wanted to swim. *Where?* He didn't know. There must be someplace, right?

Then he acknowledged that he had been born in Kuwait. Did he speak Arabic? Some. But he'd left when he was a child. What other languages? The usual: English, French, a little Spanish, and German, of course.

Who could doubt him? He looked like a tourist; the yellow shirt with blue parrots was nearly a cliché. But the remarkable thing about this German who'd exiled himself from his family because it was too cold up there in Germany in July was the depth and breadth of his knowledge about the crisis in Syria. The names of the towns and provinces rolled off his tongue like a vocabulary he'd minted himself. He steered me to websites that chronicled the beginning of the protest movement in the spring of 2011 and to photos of the boy who'd been tortured to death with an electric drill by Bashar's thugs as the uprising gained momentum. The German told me that all of this bloodletting was part of a grand Iranian strategy to enlist Russia and the United States as unlikely allies in a war against the Islamist ideologues whose dream was a unified caliphate that stretched from the mountains of Pakistan to the beaches of Tel Aviv. Iran was the true enemy of Western interests here. Didn't I understand that?

I told the German tourist I was ill-equipped to comment on such matters, but when I told him I'd made a quick trip to the Syrian border the day before, he said, "Hmm ... I might like to do that, too."

A few hours later I met a Swiss journalist who had lived nine years in Baghdad during that war, though she modestly described her Arabic as only so-so. She'd been a friend of Marie Colvin, the British journalist who'd lost sight in one eye in Sri Lanka and her life in Homs, Syria, during the terrible shelling of that city by Bashar al-Assad's forces in February.

I think it may have been the Swiss journalist's first time in Antioch, and she, too, wanted to go to the border with Henri and me. When I said a German tourist would be going with us, she cocked her head. *Tourist?* But the next day, the three of us piled into the hotel van and, with Henri at the wheel, headed once again toward Yayladağı. Henri said he'd driven one of the hotel's other vehicles for a wedding the night before. "You should have seen that car!" he said.

The German tourist had jettisoned the blue parrots and was dressed as though for safari. The Swiss journalist whispered that she'd never met a person who appeared to want so desperately to look like a journalist. If the German was one, he was probably a freelancer just like us, with nothing but our business cards to protect us from the unknown. I had not forgotten the advice a reporter had given me before I went to El Salvador for the first time: "Don't go out alone. Don't go out at night. And remember that the only people who can help you are your fellow journalists." It was the best advice I'd ever received.

Whatever his intentions, the German was one of us now.

The refugee camp at Yayladağı was filled with more than 2,500 Syrians in a multistory tobacco factory with adjoining warehouses, one of which had burst into flame five days before — a fire set by regime spies, according to some of the refugees who'd escaped just in time.

The official cause was the explosion of a gas canister used in cooking. The fire had killed two children and badly injured another six of the refugees, but the blue-and-white tents behind the burned warehouse had been spared. In fields beyond the tents stood stalks of ripening tobacco, some leaves already harvested and hanging in sheds to dry, and beyond the tobacco fields stretched apple orchards that ended just shy of the Syrian border, in the shadow of a mountain where the regime-held town of Kassab sprawled in a saddle between two green ridges under a startling Mediterranean sky.

Henri said that two years before, Kassab and other towns like it in northern Syria had been crowded with busloads of European tourists. But now there were no tourists, and the border was closed for Syrians without passports. The refugees who had fled across it anyway, sometimes through minefields or under automatic-weapons fire, had stories they wanted to tell us about what it was like on the other side.

A woman said that her son had been killed when the revolution started, and that forty-two of her neighbors had been lined up to be shot. When she tried to help, the neighbors shouted, "You'd better run for your life!" So she did. One of her friends was injured and couldn't run, so the friend, like all of the other neighbors, was shot to death, and the woman, who had by now dissolved into tears, said she could never forgive herself for leaving her friend like that.

The German was a much better translator than Henri, so I stuck close to him as a man dressed all in black said that two of his seven brothers had been killed, and as Nasir, a seventy-seven-year-old ex-boxer, challenged me to walk the twelve kilometers with him to the rebel enclave on the other side of the border. The old man was wearing sandals, a long brown dishdasha, and a red and white keffiyeh. He looked like one of those Old Testament prophets, a Malachi or Ezekiel. But then he showed me a photo of himself in his mustachioed prime: heavily built, bare-chested, and oiled to a glossy sheen. "Give me a gun!" he shouted. "I'm not afraid to fight!"

Another man, who was from Jisr al-Shughur, told me his leg had been broken in seven places by bomb fragments. When he recovered, he said he'd be going back with an AK-47, if only he could get hold of one. Others talked of murdered friends, missing relatives, elaborate regime torture methods, and the failure of the international community, in particular the United Nations, to do anything about what they called Bashar al-Assad's genocide against his own people.

And then a father of four said what I'd already heard twice before: "Nobody's helping us. All we have is God."

In the book of Matthew, Chapter 6, Jesus gives one of his most comforting, but also most paradoxical, homilies:

[30]Wherefore, if God so clothe the grass of the field, which today is, and tomorrow is cast into the oven, shall he not much more clothe you, O ye of little faith?

[31]Therefore take no thought, saying, What shall we eat? or, What shall we drink? or, Wherewithal shall we be clothed?

[32]...for your heavenly Father knoweth that ye have need of all these things.

[33]But seek ye first the kingdom of God, and his righteousness; and all these things shall be added unto you.

[34]Take therefore no thought for the morrow: for the morrow shall take thought for the things of itself. Sufficient unto the day is the evil thereof.

I wondered whether saying "All we have is God," instead of being a statement of belief, might instead be a form of prayer. The phrase reminded me of a spiritual we'd sung when I was growing up in Birmingham: "He's all I need," we'd sing. "He's all I need. All that I need."

But what if I were to sing that song to the Syrian woman whose son and neighbors had been murdered during the revolution, or to the father of four who'd fled with his family to avoid certain death and was now homeless, without adequate food and clothing, and with no secure future ahead?

I don't think Jesus ever said, "I'm all you need."

Even that encouraging parable about the birds and the lilies of the field ends with one of the most chilling sentences in the New Testament: "Sufficient unto the day is the evil thereof."

That night, the Swiss journalist told me that she was sure the tourist was a German spy. "No doubt about it," she said. "He was talking about where he lived in Munich, not realizing that I knew the neighborhood and that it was crawling with agents. They and their families all live there."

So it didn't surprise me much when he joined us at the table and said, "They're going to let me go in with them. I'm just waiting for the call." And then he told us about the other languages he knew, including Farsi and Russian, of course, and the borders he'd crossed surreptitiously: Cambodia, Iran, but the worst, he said, was Myanmar, or Burma as it was called then. "Oh, God, I thought I'd never get in there, and then I thought I'd never get out alive. I also hung out with the Mormons in Utah for a summer. Thought I might join, but decided not to."

He didn't have to say any more, although it seemed he was dying to. The smile sufficed, the practiced nonchalance. It felt better to know about him for sure, and I could tell that the Swiss journalist, who was scheduled to return to Istanbul in a couple of days, was itching to go into Syria with him.

She had to file her story before she went to bed. The German and I stayed up late and talked. It was a moment familiar to me from covering other trouble spots: crimes, riots, and natural disasters. I longed to be a part of what was going to happen next. It was the body in the pool of blood, the stretch of barrier islands where the hurricane makes landfall. It was a war, where suffering and faith were inevitable, and I was drawn to it for those very reasons.

I slept through my alarm the next morning, threw my clothes into my backpack, and panicked when I didn't see the hotel van parked out front, as it always was. "My God, I gotta catch that bus," I told the woman at the front desk.

"Don't worry," she said. "I'll call Henri...oh, there he is now. Have a pleasant trip, Mr. Covington, and do come back to see us!"

I thanked her, feeling as if she'd saved my life, then walked outside to find a grinning Henri, but still no van.

"What are you worried about?" Henri said. He'd been talking to the owner of the pet store next door. "We're going in this!" He pointed to a candy-apple-red VW convertible, a 1973 model, he'd later tell me. The top of the Beetle was down. A white bow was attached to the front trunk lid, and long white streamers were attached to the sides and rear. The streamers appeared to be made of lace.

"I drove the bride and groom in this! Isn't it something?"

I didn't care about the bride and groom. I didn't care about how we got to the bus station. I just told Henri to drive as fast as he could—a mistake, of course. This VW didn't have seat belts. It did have an FM radio, though, and the radio happened to be tuned to a Turkish news station. "What's he talking about?" I asked Henri.

"Nothing! Just Syria!" he shouted.

Great.

But when a Turkish translator for the network began talking over the thin voice of a European speaking in English, Henri and I together were able to get the gist. It was a Monday in July of 2012, the day the International Red Cross seemed to be confirming what everybody had suspected for months: that the popular revolution in Bashar al-Assad's Syria was now a civil war: a war between brothers, the worst kind of all.

Henri had stopped at a red light. When we started up again, he said, "Hey, look to your right!"

I saw a woman in an *abaya,* a *niqab,* and black gloves. She was wearing goggles over the veil, and she was riding a moped. "Have you ever seen anything as funny as that?" Henri asked.

I thought about the two old guys riding in a candy-apple-red VW convertible with lace streamers blowing in the wind, and said: "What do you think she thinks about us?"

. . .

Next day I learned about the bomb that had exploded at the National Security building in Damascus, killing the regime's defense minister and Bashar's brother-in-law, who happened to be deputy defense minister. Another general, a former defense minister, had also been killed.

When I finally got to Istanbul, I called the Swiss journalist. She said something big was in the works along the border; she'd heard artillery fire. And when she called the next day, she sounded like she'd been mainlining amphetamines. "You wouldn't believe it! The rebels have taken four border crossings, including Bab al-Hawa, the one opposite Reyhanlı!"

"Did you go?"

"Yes, yes. The artillery had stopped, but when we got over there, the place looked like Baghdad in 2003. It was incredible. And I'm the only journalist from a German-language newspaper who's here!"

It sounded like the beginning of Bashar al-Assad's final days. Rumors flew in the press that he'd gone to Latakia to make his last stand.

I regretted having missed the sound of artillery and the sight of the blasted ruins of the border crossing at Bab al-Hawa, but it wasn't my story. It belonged to the Swiss journalist. I didn't know what my story was yet, but I knew I would call my younger daughter from the rooftop of the hotel in Istanbul at midnight my time, four in the afternoon hers, and hold my phone up into the air so she could hear what it was like when Ramadan began and the mosques in this city of twenty million people would issue their call to prayer at the same time. It would be like nothing in the world either one of us had ever heard before, or were likely to hear again. I also knew that I'd be back in Antioch as soon as I could find the money to get there, although I wouldn't be able to promise my daughters that I wouldn't cross the border this time.

7

The Disappeared

What man of you, having an hundred sheep, if he lose
one of them, doth not leave the ninety and nine in the
wilderness, and go after that which is lost, until he find it?

—Luke 15:4

Four months later, in November of 2012, I was standing in line at
a grocery store in Lubbock when the cashier, a young student,
asked what I was doing for Thanksgiving.

"I'm going to Turkey," I said.

"Oh, that'll be nice."

"I hope so. It's a long way from here."

"Turkey?" she said. "I bet it's not more than two and a half hours.
Do you have family there?"

That's when it occurred to me that she must be talking about the
town of Turkey, Texas, and yes, it was about a two-hour drive.

"I'm sorry," I said. "I meant the country Turkey."

"Oh." She nodded, and then smiled. "Do you want stamps or ice
with your purchase?" she asked.

I shook my head.

"Sonny!" she shouted. "Help on register four!"

"That's okay," I said. "I can manage." I had only two bags, mostly
snacks for the plane. I knew I should have asked for paper instead of
plastic, for environmental reasons, but the plastic bags were useful
in picking up and discarding what my dog left behind on her morning and evening walks.

"You have a nice night, sir," the young cashier said. "And drive safely on that trip to Turkey."

"I'm not driving. The Turkey where I'm going is almost halfway around the world."

"I bet it is." She smiled again, but she was already ringing up groceries out of the next customer's cart.

"I don't think you understand," I added.

"Oh, I do. I know what you mean. Turkey for Thanksgiving. That's funny."

I knew I was making a nuisance of myself, but I couldn't seem to help it. The customer behind me in line was starting to get annoyed, so I finally turned to go. But before I got to the grocery store's enormous glass doors, they opened automatically with a *swoosh,* and by some miraculous coincidence my Turkish-language teacher, Mehmet, walked in.

"*Iyi akşamlar,*" he said. "We've been missing you."

I took his elbow and addressed the checkout girl. "Look. See? This is my teacher. He's teaching me Turkish."

She smiled back at me.

"Are you still going to Istanbul?" Mehmet asked. He was a faculty member in mechanical engineering, a very fine man who had donated his time to school me in a language that I would never, ever understand or be able to speak more than two words of.

"Yes. I fly out tomorrow," I told him in a voice loud enough for the cashier to hear.

To this day I don't know who had been having more fun with whom, the young cashier with me or me with her.

I let Mehmet know I was sorry I had missed our last few classes. I had been teaching a full load that semester and auditing introductory Arabic, another language I would never be able to understand or speak. Arabic, I told him, was killing me.

"Oh, yes. Arabic is very difficult," he said. "Well, you must tell us all about your trip when you get back. *Guvenli seyahat.* Travel safely, Professor."

"Iyi gejeler," I replied, and then realized I'd screwed up that exchange, too. Instead of simply saying goodbye, I had just told Mehmet that I was going to bed.

The next morning, the Friday before Thanksgiving, I again left Texas for the Middle East. My flight from Istanbul to Hatay (the airport that served Antioch) arrived at 1:40 in the morning. It had been packed with bearded young Sunnis who looked like they were headed to the Syrian civil war. In the terminal they stood quietly in small groups around the baggage conveyor belt until it cranked up, and when it did, their minimal belongings came out tightly packed, unlike the suitcases, garment bags, and electronic goods the other passengers had brought home from Istanbul or from visits to foreign capitals. If these were indeed potential fighters, they might be able to purchase the other items they needed at one of the numerous army surplus stores that had clustered around the *dolmuş* (minibus) station in Antioch and, I'd been told, were mostly owned, ironically, by Alevis. Weapons might be provided for the fighters once they crossed into northern Syria, although from what I'd heard from the young men in Güveççi or in front of the refugee camp in Yayladağı, nobody was being provided very much of anything from anywhere.

Like many of the passengers on the airplane, the cabdriver from the airport also seemed a different sort this time. He spoke only Arabic, an indication that he was probably a recent arrival in the city. The competition was intense among cabdrivers, and the two I'd used briefly the previous summer were Turks whose Arabic was limited or nonexistent. So I was nervous coming into the city at the darkest time of a November night in a cab driven by an Arab fingering his prayer beads. I didn't know the layout of the city well enough to tell whether we were actually on the right road or not.

A few polite phrases in Arabic, though, and the driver's response convinced me that there was nothing to worry about. He dropped me off at the Liwan, where I learned that I'd mistakenly made my reservation for the following night and that the hotel was full. The night clerk booked me at another hotel down the street. He had to run down there to rouse someone, and when he came back, he told me it was a more expensive room, but that the Liwan would cover the difference and that they were looking forward to having me back for the rest of my stay.

"This is your home," he said with a wide smile. "I learn you Turkish. You learn me English."

The next morning, when I returned to the Liwan and got my room key, I noticed that Henri was seated at the computer screen in the bar. I figured he was playing a video game, but when he saw me, he motioned me over. "Look at this," he said. "It's about Güveççi."

The broadcast was from Channel D in Istanbul, and the newscaster was a woman. I asked what she was saying.

The translation to English was too much for Henri, so he found a text report from another source and translated it using Google. Ignoring the lunacies of machine translation, I got a sense of what had happened. According to the report, panicked residents of Güveççi had been awakened before dawn by the sound of automatic-weapons fire and the explosion of a tank round in a nearby field as Syrian army soldiers, including another general, tried to defect to Turkey along the same route used by civilian refugees. Turkish artillery from the fort above Güveççi had returned fire.

Maybe Turkey and Syria were on the brink of war, so Henri and I headed out again to that border town forty minutes from Antioch. When Henri turned off the paved highway onto the familiar rutted dirt road, he said the news report was probably nothing. A stray tank round, a little artillery fire, it happened all the time. "But who knows?" he added.

Güveççi didn't look like a war zone when we arrived. The town's schoolchildren were on the playground. They were dressed in typical Turkish school uniforms—blue pants for the boys and long blue skirts for the girls; both boys and girls wore brocaded blue shirts with white collars. A woman on the street in front of the school told us that her children, but not their teacher, had heard the explosion of the tank round. As we spoke with her, a teaching assistant began ushering the children into the one-room school. I hoped our presence hadn't caused her to do this, but we followed her inside nonetheless, trying to find out what she had heard. Instead of answering our questions, she referred us to the teacher.

We stood in an alcove outside the classroom and tried to get the teacher's attention. Impeccably dressed in a white shirt, tie, sweater vest, and slacks, he was watching as the children settled into their seats. When he finally turned our way and we asked if he or the children had heard an explosion that morning before dawn, he shook his head vigorously. We thanked him for his time, but as we turned to leave, he stepped out of the classroom and into the alcove. His expression, which had been rigid in front of the children, melted when he reached us.

"Yes, the children heard it," he said in a softer, measured voice that suggested how very much they'd heard since this war began.

I thought of a morning in Alabama when my daughters were in elementary school. I was going to drive them there, but we had just stepped out of the house when we heard an explosion.

They both turned to me. "What was that?" they asked in unison.

"Thunder."

"Dad," the older one said, "there's not a cloud in the sky."

"Must have been a sonic boom, then, a jet high up where we can't see."

The sound of a bomb had not been uncommon in Birmingham when I was their age, but I didn't want to frighten them, so I just took them to school. Afterward I learned that the sound came from a bomb that had gone off in front of an abortion clinic just a mile and a half away from our house. The homemade device had killed an off-duty policeman whose job it was to provide security for the clinic, and it had horribly injured a nurse who worked there, driving nails, tiny ball bearings, and other metal debris into her face and body.

When the girls found out, they weren't surprised. They told me they knew I was lying in order to ease their fear, but they were not babies anymore. They could take the truth, even if it was the worst kind.

Henri and I never found the spot in Güveççi where the regime's tank shell had exploded. As we walked down a goat path lined with fig trees and pines toward the pastures at the barbed wire that marked the border, we heard small-arms fire from the other side, so we turned around and walked back up.

I didn't tell Henri, or anyone else, that I wanted to find a way to cross the border into northern Syria without resorting to the smuggling trails that journalists had been obliged to use until then, and I was dead sure that the German and the Swiss journalist had been able to get across some other way. How else could she have seen the wreckage of Bab al-Hawa, the Syrian crossing opposite Reyhanlı? I also remembered that Henri had told me he planned to take them up to Kilis, another border town in the mountains, on the very afternoon he had driven me to the bus station in the VW convertible, so that was the first question I put to him when we got back to the Liwan: Had he taken the Swiss journalist and the German to Kilis?

"Yes, I took *her*," he said. "The German guy didn't go. He's CIA, you know. He's not staying at the hotel anymore, but he's still in Antioch. We see him around all the time."

The spy game was one I played, too, of course. It made our lives more exciting than they really were. The women who worked at the Liwan, for instance, were convinced that the Irish businessman who said he sold home furnishings was actually with Israel's Mossad. "His address is Tel Aviv," one of the women would whisper, "and he doesn't look Irish at all."

"His business must be doing pretty good for him to stay here all the time," another of them would say.

"Yes, but the only people he talks to in the café are young Syrian men who don't look like they're in the market for fancy furniture."

They would nod and smile at the end of conversations like these.

I had no idea why they let me eavesdrop, unless they were sure I wouldn't be the man who would inform on them or slit their throats in the night.

But I still didn't tell Henri I wanted to cross the border. I told him only that I wanted to step into the no-man's-land between the two countries, to get a sense of the terrifying vacuum that must exist there. However, I also had to ask myself whether I wanted to cross the border just so I could say that I had.

The only American I'd heard of who had disappeared in Syria was a freelance journalist named Austin Tice. He'd been kidnapped by unknown assailants, presumably members of Bashar's militia group, the *shabiha,* on August 12, 2012. Tice was a former Marine officer and experienced combat journalist who had put his life on the line to get the story. I didn't yet know about the second American free-lancer who'd disappeared, Peter Theo Curtis, who'd been kidnapped in October by Jabhat al-Nusra, the al-Qaeda-linked rebel group.

I did know that freelancers were for the most part the only West-erners getting the story. The risk was considerable. But once you know you're going to die in a shit-filled ditch in El Salvador, you're no longer afraid to die, or at least that's what I was telling myself. Who knew what I would do if I crossed the border, or how I would feel about it, or what I would find out if and when I did it—until, and unless, I did it.

The crossing at Yayladağı proved out of the question. Henri and I were waved away before we even got close. I got a little farther at the crossing at Reyhanlı, twenty minutes from Antioch, with the help of a local cabdriver. He and I cleared the first obstacle, but the Turkish police at the second checkpoint turned me back when he told them I was a professor at the same moment I was saying that I was a jour-nalist. Apparently you can't be both in Turkey. It didn't add up.

"Just let me get as close as I can to Syria," I said. "I'm a writer. I'll probably never have the opportunity to be here again."

I was told I would have to enter the building and ask the enormous man toward the end of an otherwise deserted hallway. And by enormous, I mean a replica of himself but half a size larger.

He spoke absolutely perfect English. "No. You can't go any farther. It's too dangerous."

"Just let me look. Two minutes."

"No."

"Cross my heart. Two minutes."

He finally nodded, and when I walked to the end of the hall and emerged into the sunlight, I seemed to be looking into a prison yard of some kind. I couldn't make sense of it. There were plenty of people on the other side of the fence, Syrians I guessed, all men, it seemed, but I didn't know who they were or what their status might be.

Then I heard footsteps behind me. "Okay, your two minutes are up." It was the giant again.

"Can I ask you a couple of questions?" I said.

"No, and if you don't leave right now, I'll have you arrested."

That worked. I'd seen *Midnight Express* in college, the film that for decades had ruined Turkey for me, as it had for a generation of other American men.

Henri had been waiting patiently in the parking lot. He was glad I'd seen whatever it was I wanted to see.

"You said you took the Swiss journalist to Kilis? Is it far?" I asked.

"Maybe four hours, maybe less. It's up in the mountains. I know the superintendent of the refugee camp there, so if you ever want to go into the camp, there's no problem."

I said sure, I'd like to go to the refugee camp, but that's all I told him about my plans.

Suddenly, or so it seemed, it was Thanksgiving Day 2012, and I did what every American in a foreign country might be tempted to do. I went to the nearest mall. The one in Antioch, Prime Mall, was shaped exactly like the mother ship in *Close Encounters of the Third Kind*. Inside, it opened onto an enormous atrium, four stories high, with an ice rink on the bottom floor, movie theaters on the fourth, and stores in between, some of them clearly American-oriented, including a McDonald's, of course. I couldn't help it. It was Thanksgiving. I ordered a double cheeseburger with fries and a large Coke.

Two days later, on a gray Saturday morning, Henri and I set out for Kilis. It rained all the way, but it was a soft, light rain, and the air seemed not much cooler than it would have been in the stands at a college football game back home in Alabama or Texas. Occasionally we'd see an ambulance weaving its way through the scores of tractor-trailer rigs or flocks of sheep, their shepherds on horseback atop colorful saddle pads, cell phones in hand. The ambulance was probably headed to the Turkish government hospital in Antioch, and its occupant was probably Syrian, either a Free Syrian Army fighter or, more likely at this point in the war, a civilian: a woman or child. Around this time, the Syrian Observatory for Human Rights was estimating that three-quarters of the 38,000 dead during the war had been civilians.

Once we'd cleared the the semis, the drive was spectacular: on one side of the highway were fields of cherry, olive, and pistachio trees that stretched in straight or gently curving rows all the way to the horizon, where they disappeared among low-hung clouds. On the other side of the highway stood the multiple minarets and silver domes of mosques that dotted every Turkish town or city. One distant town in particular looked like a miniature piece of Moorish exotica, but when the clouds behind it lifted and the massive, snow-covered mountains loomed into view, the effect was both frightening and exhilarating. I told Henri I could live in a place like that, and he reminded me that I might want to change my religion first.

And then the road to Kilis forked off from the main highway, became a two-lane, and started its long, twisting ascent up the mountains. The trip proved longer than I had expected, but there were enough spectacular views to make the time go faster. Kilis itself was much larger than I had anticipated. There was a sparkling new university on a hilltop at the edge of town, and high-rise apartment buildings and traffic circles in the center. Even the bus station appeared to be new, and the Oncupinar border crossing, five kilometers to the south, was uncrowded and orderly, particularly compared to the one at Reyhanlı.

Henri assumed I was there to visit the large, showcase refugee camp to the right of the border crossing, the Canister Camp, so called because families lived in metal structures instead of tents and had paved roads, a school, a clinic, and a mosque. But I insisted that first I wanted to see how rigorously Turkish authorities were controlling the border itself.

As it turned out, they didn't seem to be controlling it at all. They stamped my passport with hardly a word, waved me on at the police station, and after a one-mile walk in a light mist, I saw the billboard that read "Free Syria Wellcame You." I wrote in my notebook "I am in Syria."

I had entered the country alone, without a translator, guide, or colleague. There appeared to be no border formalities at the Syrian crossing, which was called Bab al-Salameh, only a crowd of men milling about, looking for work or waiting for relatives to deliver food, medicine, or diapers from the Turkish side. They knew that the Turkish camps were full, so the only Syrian refugees allowed to enter Turkey would be the ones with passports issued by the regime of Bashar al-Assad, a requirement that eliminated the vast majority of refugees, because they were the ones who happened to be fleeing that regime.

The refugee camp on the Syrian side of the border was a crowded, muddy, and ill-smelling tent city. I didn't want to stay there, so I picked out the oldest, thinnest man in the most decrepit pickup and asked him to give me a ride to the nearest town. The old man's name was Ammar, and he was not as old as I'd first thought, merely grizzled and turkey-necked, like me. It was a short hop to the town of Azaz, the Tomb of Tanks, so named because it had been the site of the first rebel victory during the war. I knew that the town and its surroundings had been bombed and strafed on a regular basis ever since, and I'd seen photos of the open graves that were routinely dug in neat rows in anticipation of the next attack.

I also knew that the terrorist group Jabhat al-Nusra might be there. But I was convinced by what I'd read that the residents of Azaz considered themselves free men and women, and that was a precious, reassuring factor in my favor.

Besides, there were places Ammar wanted me to see: the ruined mosque, regime tanks disabled or buried in the rubble, the concrete skeleton that had once been the town's bus station, and the neighborhoods with streets that seemed to go on forever in jumbles of masonry and twisted steel rods. At least one store was open, though, so we watched as residents queued up for cooking oil and kerosene. The only man in sight with an AK-47 that day was the one directing traffic in the center of what the residents called Martyrs Square. Ammar said that the fighters had gone south to liberate the highway between Aleppo and Homs, and I could tell by his voice and gestures that he was proud of them.

Finally, he took me on a roundabout route with no traffic and few sites of interest, clearly not the one by which we'd arrived. It was a practice in Syria with which I'd soon become familiar. The road ended in a T intersection. Ammar pointed to the right and said, "Aleppo?"

Then he pointed to the left and said, "Turkey?"

I thought hard about that, but finally said, "Turkey."

Getting out of Syria, though, was not as easy as getting in. I hadn't had to get my passport stamped on entry, but at the exit point passport control was well set up, and the line was long, the heat and odor of perspiration suffocating. For some reason, a clerk took my passport while I was still far away from the counter. I thought this might be a courtesy to hurry my exit along, since I was clearly a foreigner and possibly sympathetic to their cause. But as the men ahead of me got their passports stamped, mine was examined by several people. I motioned for them to give it back so I could have it stamped, but still they kept it. They were whispering among themselves. When it was my turn in line, the clerk told me to stand aside and wait. I pointed out that the man in back of him had my passport, but he didn't acknowledge what I'd said. About that time four men with dark, full beards entered the building. One of them retrieved my passport and motioned for me to go with them, two in front of me and two behind.

We walked out into the graying afternoon. It was still drizzling and noticeably cold. I wished I had brought a heavier coat. I wondered, of course, where the men were taking me, but I assumed it would be to ask me questions, I didn't want to think what kind. It occurred to me briefly that they might belong to al-Nusra and that the questions might be the sort for which no answers were expected. There might not be questions at all.

The room they took me to was in a small building across the road. It had a desk and three chairs. Paneled, I believe. Without windows, I believe. The man with my passport disappeared into another room, and I reached out to stop him — as though I could. But one of the others, the one nearest the desk, said in halting English, "Don't worry."

He motioned for me to sit, which I did, but I wasn't fully convinced until the man who had taken my passport came back and gave it to me. A relatively clean-shaven young man behind him said, "We have a copy machine. We just wanted a copy." He introduced himself as Anas, said he'd Googled me and that he was happy I was there. Then he handed me a card. It was embossed with the Free Syrian flag, and it read "Azaz Media Center" in bold script. He said they had just opened this office. I was among the first American journalists to be welcomed there.

So we had tea, Anas gave me his e-mail address and phone number, and I left in those high spirits familiar to hikers who have recognized the sign on a tree they have marked and know now that they're on the right trail.

Henri was furious when I got back to the Turkish side. "You've been gone more than five hours!" he shouted. "Where have you been?"

"Azaz," I said.

"You went into Syria? Are you crazy?"

"Maybe, but now let's go to the Canister Camp."

"It's too late for that. And you owe me for all the time you were gone."

"Sure. Can we do the camp next time?"

By now he was smiling. "Okay, okay," he said. "You're lucky. You know that, don't you?"

I told him I did. And as we descended onto the well-ordered Turkish agricultural plain, so distant from the cold drizzle of Azaz and the wreckage of war, I knew I had the photo I'd come for: it was of a proud boy on the top of a Syrian army tank. He wore red pants, his feet planted firmly apart until he cocked one leg in defiance. His left hand was stretched out and down by his side, as though to ward off an unseen enemy, and his other hand was giving the world a crisp, Free Syrian salute.

I did not know at the time that the American journalist James Foley, along with a British colleague named John Cantlie, had disappeared on Thanksgiving Day just an hour's drive away from Azaz. Foley would be held hostage and tortured for two years by the Islamic State of Iraq and al-Sham (ISIS). ISIS was a terror group that had originated as al-Qaeda in Iraq and would be linked to al-Qaeda's Syrian franchise, al-Nusra, until Osama bin Ladin's successor, Ayman al-Zawahiri, cut ties with ISIS because they were too violent even for al-Qaeda. During those two years brave men and women would be searching for Foley and his colleague. I would meet several of them—American, European, and Syrian—and his family would never give up hope.

They would call for a Global Moment of Silence or Prayer for their son on July 25, 2013, the Feast Day of St. James, and even after his beheading by ISIS in August of 2014, their faith would persist. "We just thank God for the gift of Jim," his mother would say. She and her husband understood what some other Americans might not have understood at the time. In his work as a witness to war, James Foley had entered into the suffering of others, a definition of faith as clear as any in the Gospel of Jesus Christ.

So had Steven Sotloff, David Haines, Alan Henning, Peter Kassig, Kayla Mueller, and the many other journalists and humanitarian aid workers who had disappeared, been kidnapped, or killed. Their particular religions and beliefs were immaterial, except in the light of how those individuals wanted their work to be seen.

I began to wonder what my search for faith was about. Was I merely an aging narcissist who was willing to take risks in order to get just one more story before he checked out for good? It was a question that would haunt me every day on my travels to the Turkish-Syrian border and beyond, and it would persist even to the end, as I drove to Arizona on that night in the spring of 2014 in search of Kayla Mueller's parents.

But there was another question that I knew the answer to. Would I have walked into northern Syria alone if I had known that two Western journalists, including an American like me, had been kidnapped there two days before?

Yes. Of course I would have. As would they.

8

The Headless Girl

But Jesus said, Suffer little children, and forbid them not,
to come unto me: for of such is the kingdom of heaven.

—*Matthew 19:14*

In 2012, *New York Times* correspondent C. J. Chivers posted the
link to a video the likes of which I'd never seen before. Uploaded
by Syrian activists, the video purported to show the aftermath of a
regime bombing of Kafr Owaid in Idlib Province, and it opened with
the bloodied face of an adult corpse. Beside that corpse were the
bodies of three small boys lying in their own blood. "A massacre,"
said a voice off camera.

When the camera panned back past the adult corpse to a nearby
green blanket with an intricate design, a man's hand had barely
begun to reveal what was under it before other voices said, "Cover
the woman. Show him the little girl."

The man moved on to a black blanket piled in the corner of the
room. His hand hesitated, as though the suggestion of the others
might have been improper. But once he made his decision, he pulled
back the blanket and carefully lifted up a tiny girl who was wearing
a blue pinafore with ruffled white sleeves and hem. The man's grief-
stricken face was visible now as he brought the girl toward the camera. It was clear she had been recently killed, because her arms and
legs still dangled in a natural way. Rigor mortis had not yet set in. It
was as though she were still alive, sleeping perhaps, and might wake
up at any moment. But there was one problem. The girl had no head.

The man had decided that no matter the moral or privacy issues involved, the world needed to see this. "We bring our case before God," he said. "Before God alone. For mankind has failed us."

I would have liked for the world to see the first patient I met at a hospital in Reyhanlı, Turkey, a stone's throw from the Syrian border. I'll call this girl Aini, the Arabic word for spring. She was twelve years old. Her room was painted a bright pink and was small, particularly since there were five people crowded into it. Her nurse would serve as my interpreter, and her physical therapist spoke a little English, too. Aini's mother was also in the room, where she'd been since Aini had been admitted, and Aini herself lay in the bed in a white knit top and oversized diapers.

Her eyes were large and deep brown, her hair cut short, perhaps to make it easier to attend to. The physical therapist dabbed her forehead with a damp cloth and whispered, smiling, into her ear. But Aini never smiled at all. As introductions went around the room, I was surprised by the enthusiasm with which her mother greeted me. I couldn't imagine such a thing happening in my own country, where strangers of any kind, especially foreigners, would not be welcomed into the room of an injured child.

Aini's story was told by her mother, elaborated on by the physical therapist, and translated by the nurse. Occasionally they all laughed when the details didn't match, all but Aini. She didn't move a muscle during the telling, not even her eyes.

The essence of the story was straightforward. Aini and her father had been walking along a street in a small town in Idlib Province when they were both shot by a sniper. Her father died instantly. Aini was taken to a nearby hospital, but the doctors there couldn't remove the bullet, and the hospital they took her to next was bombed by Bashar's air force. The family was able to escape with the help of the Free Syrian Army, but Aini's brothers, of whom there were seven, had disappeared along the way. Nobody knew where they were or even whether they were still alive.

The physical therapist said the bullet was out now, but that it had severed Aini's spinal cord at the T6-T7 level, an area of the spine at which paraplegia would be the likely result. He said that Aini's prognosis was grim. In addition to the physical injury, there was the psychological one. Aini's mother told me her daughter hadn't spoken for four months after the death of her father. She had only recently begun to say a few words.

I asked them to ask her if she had a message for the people of America.

Aini's expression did not change as she spoke, and her answer was no less grave for being predictable: "I just want them to help me walk again."

For the first time I felt that what I was doing along the border might be useful, if only to transmit a message from a young girl whose life had been forever changed on a day when she was doing nothing more unusual than walking with her father down a quiet street in their hometown.

When I left Aini's room, her doctor, whom I'll call Miran, walked close beside me down the hall, past rooms with other seriously injured children, and held my elbow as we descended a flight of stairs. The landing opened onto an outer courtyard that had been swept clean and was filled with bright sunlight. There I asked him if he thought Aini would ever walk again. The look in his eyes said no, and he squeezed my elbow before releasing it.

Miran seemed too young to be a doctor, and I told him so. He smiled and said he'd been in his residency at the University of Aleppo when he decided to join the peaceful antiregime protests in the spring of 2011. Those protests had begun in the university town of Dara'a, fifty miles south of Damascus, after children had scrawled antigovernment slogans on a wall. He said Bashar's much-feared secret police, the Mukhabarat, had taken the children into custody and subjected them to torture. The violent part of the uprising started when the protesters discovered that their families and children were being murdered. "Nobody was helping the protesters," he said, "and something had to be done."

When I asked Miran to tell me about the most difficult procedure he'd had to perform in Syria, he said it wasn't in a hospital of any kind. It was at night, in a house without electricity in Aleppo.

"He was a fifteen-year-old boy with gunshot wounds to his head and thigh," Miran said. "I had to sterilize a pair of scissors over a fire. Someone held a flashlight. I used the scissors to remove the bullets. There was no anesthesia. Nothing."

When I asked whether the patient had survived, he said he didn't know, but he doubted it.

"Sometimes we cry because we don't know what to do for these people," he said, "and even if we did, we wouldn't have the suitable equipment." The few doctors left in northern Syria were either being killed or arrested, he said. Many of them were young and hadn't specialized yet. "But there's no choice," he added. "You have to do it, even if you don't have enough experience."

I was thinking about Aini, and he must have known that.

"Frankly," he said, "sometimes I just want to go to a far-off place and live a long time and not think about Syria, but we have to stay. You understand what I mean, don't you? We have to stay."

I nodded and thanked him for talking to me. He touched his forehead and his heart, the Islamic blessing that accompanies both hello and goodbye, and then he turned and went about his work.

After that, all I have to say is that I was not much moved by the Christmas Day service at the Eastern Orthodox Church in Antioch. It was more than just not understanding the language or the order of worship or the significance of the extravagant ecclesiastical garments the bishops wore. It was the fact that the level of security at the church was intrusive and frustrating. The reason was valid, of course, since this was the largest Christian congregation in a vastly Muslim city, and tensions had been increasing to such an extent that within the next three months, two Eastern Orthodox bishops would disappear on the road from Aleppo to the Turkish border. Their driver, a deacon in the church, would be executed on the spot.

It seemed as if Christians, in their sense of isolation, had started to turn on one another. Gaining entrance to these churches during an ordinary week was often impossible. Since I knew some of the families who attended the Antioch Protestant Church, I was welcomed there. But strangers might not have been.

"Did you bring your guns?" an old man asked me at the door.

I smiled, thinking he must be joking.

"We have ours," he said in a voice that let me know he wasn't.

My feeling about church had always been "Open up the gates... let whoever wishes to, partake." Of course, that's a romanticized version of what really went on in our white Protestant churches in Birmingham when I was a child. I remember the day my father came back from a Board of Stewards meeting to tell us that our pastor had solved the problem of what to do if a Negro happened to enter the church one Sunday. "We'll just be courteous and do what we'd do to anybody else who enters like that. We'll take him by the arm and escort him down the aisle, past the choir loft, and out the back door." The imitation Dad did of our pastor, the tilting of his head and the sympathetic grin, was spot on.

In Antioch I tried, I really tried, to get into the spirit of that service at the Orthodox Church. The closest I came to it, though, was when the white doves were released at the end of the service and flew in a spiral up through clouds of incense that must have extended the sweet smell, like fingers of scent, into the light that fell from the cupola, a melding of the natural and the immaterial, the man and the ghost who inhabited him.

I made a quick trip into Aleppo in March; then I went back to Texas to finish the spring semester at my university. I'd made a plane reservation to return to Antioch on May 13. I hoped to visit Aini again in Reyhanlı, but on May 12 my brother Gary was rushed from his nursing home to the emergency room. He had pneumonia, and the doctors warned me he might not survive it. I canceled my flight. That was the morning I saw the news that twin car bombs had exploded in Reyhanlı, killing 52 people, including 5 children, and injuring more than 140 of all ages. A Turkish newspaper later called it "the deadliest single act of terrorism that has ever occurred on Turkish soil."

Articles online carried photos of the bombs' horrendous aftermath. Both devices had gone off in the center of town, one near the main post office and another next to the city hall. The hospital where Aini was a patient was not that far from either. Gary recovered from the pneumonia, the semester ended, and when I got back to Turkey exactly a month after the attack, I went straight to Reyhanlı and was overjoyed to see that not only had Aini not been further injured, but she was sitting up in bed. Her hair had grown out, she was wearing a Gangnam T-shirt, and when she saw me at the door she flashed a beautiful smile and gave me the peace sign.

Aini couldn't walk but she was going to survive, and she was expecting a visitor from down the hall. He wheeled himself in one-handed, a bright-eyed ten-year-old boy who'd lost his right leg and the use of his left hand. He'd also lost his brother and mother when their house was bombed, but he, too, was wearing a grin, even though I think he might have been a little peeved that Aini's wheelchair, which was folded up in the corner, was bigger than his. Suddenly I just didn't want to hear the phrase "lost generation of Syrian children" anymore.

The word *lost* suggested they were irretrievable, could never be found, and so needn't be thought about any longer. But these two had lives ahead of them. They were resilient, full of spunk. All they needed in order to have a fine future, I thought, was to stay as far away as possible from that lousy war and to finish their childhoods in a place that offered decent medical care, educational opportunities, and most of all: safety. America and its allies should long since have provided no-fly zones and protected humanitarian corridors for children like them, but it wasn't too late for the ones in northern Syria who were left.

Aini's mother had good news. All of her seven sons were alive. They were living in a cave just across the border in Idlib Province, and one of them was able to sneak across into Turkey every few days to get supplies for them. She was still worried, of course, but the news had given her hope, something that had been in short supply after her husband had been killed and her daughter had been rendered paraplegic.

She wanted me to sit down. She offered me her chair. She wished she had some food or tea to give me. She was scurrying around that little hospital room, her hands clasped in front of her as though there were some treat for me if only she could find it. I motioned for her to please sit back down. I could stay only a moment. After the nurse left, this communication was being accomplished with sign language and facial expressions, but these make for rich exchanges when life has made a turn for the better, even if it's just a little better, and even if it might not last. Her sons were still in terrible danger, she had no place to live except this hospital room, and she had no food or drink except what the staff shared with her, but she had faith.

The third time I went to see Aini, she wasn't there. The nurse told me that she and her mother had found a place to live in Reyhanlı. Her mother was doing needlework for clients and somehow getting by. Aini had become a terror with her wheelchair. The sons were still living in the cave on the other side of the border, but they were healthy and so far able to stay clear of the fighting. Maybe, just maybe, the family would be reunited in Turkey someday. Maybe, someday, the war would end and they could all go back to Syria if they wanted to. Start anew. Wouldn't that be "the substance of things hoped for"?

Unfortunately, some of the patients I saw on that visit might never be leaving the hospital. One of them was a seventy-one-year-old woman of unearthly beauty who'd been injured by one of Bashar's barrel bombs. Her legs had been amputated below her hips. The attendants had somehow managed to prop her up in bed so she could look out the window with her fixed, dignified gaze. Her head scarf was a colorful geometric print. Two other women patients who shared her room had been injured in similar attacks, and they wanted to tell me what had happened to them, so I listened. But the woman looking out the window did not want to talk about any of that, so I left her in peace.

The final time I visited the hospital, Aini's old room had been painted blue and was occupied by two boys. One of them was fourteen and had been burned by a barrel bomb in Aleppo two months before as he was walking to get ice cream. The other was a thirteen-year-old. His left hand had been blown off, the cross-sectioned bones of his forearm visible in the middle of the unbandaged stump. Two fingers on his other hand were missing. It looked as though that hand had suffered a severe burn, and although the boy wasn't smiling, his father was there, sitting on the bed and holding his son's injured hand gingerly as though it were a priceless piece of art.

Across the hall was a ten-year-old. He'd also been the victim of a barrel bomb, dropped while he was playing with a friend beside his house in Aleppo. His blanket was pulled up to his chin. I don't think he wanted me to see the injury that had occurred four months before. Since then he'd been staying at the hospital and receiving daily physical therapy while accompanied by his mother.

Suddenly I heard a commotion from the end of the hall, so I excused myself and headed to a corner room where an eight-year-old girl named Husna stood at the bedside of her friend Lutfi, who was seven and had been left paraplegic by the explosion of an artillery shell in Deir al-Zour. Husna had been poking fun at Lutfi, and both were laughing hysterically when I entered the room. Husna was lithe, a young athlete perhaps, and her hair was cropped like a boy's. From the back she looked like Peter Pan. But when she turned to me, still laughing, her face was a river of burn scars, like tributaries starting at her forehead and branching down each cheek. One eye was displaced a bit by scar tissue. But other than the scars, she seemed a normal eight-year-old. Her ears were pierced, a bright metal stud in the lobe of each one, and when she saw me, she giggled and raced down the hall and back, yelling that she had a visitor. On her return, she put her hands to her face, then opened them and shouted "Boo!" before running down the hall and back again, beside herself with what must have been, despite everything, the joy of being young and alive.

The nurse said that Husna and her mother had been in their house, her mother about to take a shower, when a rocket or bomb from an airplane hit and ignited the barrel of heating oil on their roof. The explosion and flames set Husna on fire and buried shrapnel in her body, and her recovery had been incredibly long and painful. She was an only child, and the nurse thought she and her mother had done a remarkable job of enduring the excruciating circumstances of her injury. But there was yet another source of pain for them. Husna's father was missing. He'd been working on road construction the day of the attack. He'd been detained by the regime and had not been seen or heard from since.

9

The Call

The reason I'd had to put my brother Gary into a nursing home was simple. He could no longer take care of himself. My niece, Judy, was the one who'd called. She didn't want me to tell her father, my brother-in-law Bunky, that she had.

Bunky had been looking after Gary. We had joint power of attorney, but he was older than Gary and had his own health problems. Bunky couldn't help Gary get up off the floor anymore. He'd already saved Gary's life twice by calling the police after three days without hearing from him and by forcing his way into the house the second time when he couldn't rouse him by phone. He'd also bought Gary a Life Alert device, but the thing was worthless since Gary never wore it around his neck or charged it or left it anywhere within reach.

The night I arrived in Birmingham to persuade him to come with me to Texas, he had somehow jammed his foot under the chest of drawers and couldn't get it out. He'd been able to phone Bunky, but Bunky was at a hospital where his son was in the intensive care unit, so Gary hung up without saying another word and called 911.

The police and firemen were pulling away from the house when I got there. Bunky was there, too. He'd arrived before the emergency services, but he'd left his power of attorney document at home, and Gary refused to be taken to the hospital.

The next day I packed up all of Gary's things — his clothes, papers, the family photo albums and personal items, but I left his Confederate flag on the wall. Judy could take care of that when she came to clean the house, which was in danger of being repossessed by the bank.

I finally persuaded him to get into my rental car by telling him my younger daughter had leased a very primitive garage apartment in Lubbock that she wasn't using at the time (true) and that he might be able to live there (not so true).

It was a four-day trip. At the motels along the way I took care of him, helped keep him clean, pounded his back while he coughed up phlegm, and hoped he wouldn't wander into the lobby. At some point in our journey, I asked him if he remembered hanging up on Bunky when Bunky had told him he was in the ICU with his son, Craig.

"Yeah," Gary said. "Can you believe he'd look after his son instead of me?"

When we finally got to Lubbock, I took him straight to the emergency room, something he hadn't let the police and firemen in Birmingham do. After a night's stay, attendants took him by ambulance to a nursing home I'd found, not three blocks away.

A few weeks later, Gary was rushed to another hospital with pneumonia and given a dire prognosis for recovery, but recover he did, and then he went back to the nursing home. Three or four times a week, I'd take him to eat at the Lubbock Breakfast House, then to Wal-Mart to buy a shirt and pair of slacks exactly like the ones he already had, and then, if Wal-Mart didn't have them, to CVS to buy a bag of Peanut Butter Snickers, which were not allowed at the nursing home but tolerated as long as no one fought over them. I also took him to get a haircut every week, although they cut hair at the nursing home.

The spring semester hadn't ended yet, and I would have liked to have spent more time with my daughters and grandchildren rather than with Gary, but I did my best not to mind until the usual recriminations against Dad and Bunky and me radiated out to include Jeanie and Scotty and Mom—the whole family, as though all of us could possibly have conspired to have him committed to a state mental institution.

"All of you were just a bunch of crooks."

I told him to stop talking like that, but when he continued to say that nothing had been wrong with him, nothing at all, I broke. We were at a stop sign on our way back from the errands we'd run. "Oh, really?" I said. "Nothing wrong with you?"

"No. Nothing. That's why I hated my family, and still do."

I couldn't help it. That's when I started imitating his behavior when he'd come home from the army.

I mimed biting my forearm. I yelled those strings of obscenities.

Gary burst out laughing. "What's the matter with you?" he said. "Have you lost your mind?"

Someone behind us honked. I pressed the gas pedal and made a sharp left.

"Where are you going?"

"I'm taking you back to the nursing home," I said, "and that's what I'll do every time you start talking that way about our family."

"What's your problem?" he said.

"Nothing," I said, but I had a problem all right.

My problem had stemmed from more than fifty years of pretending that nothing had been unusual about Gary's behavior. He said he hated all of us, but he'd lived in Mom and Dad's house almost all those years, even after Dad sold the one I'd grown up in and bought a much smaller one when I went off to college. Dad told me he hoped that Gary might move into a place of his own after he took a job at a company that made school binders, the same place I'd worked as a young man, but Gary never moved out, not even after he found work as a night dispatcher for the local cab company, a job he held until his retirement at sixty-five, the year Mom died.

I never doubted how much Mom and Dad loved Gary and the rest of us, so when I was ten years old and they asked me to act as though nothing was amiss in our household, I did what they said, and continued to do it even after they were both dead. But I couldn't do it anymore.

One thought allowed me to settle down and detach myself from the situation: I'd soon be back along the Turkish-Syrian border, immersing myself in the suffering of others, ignoring those at home.

Now, as I'm writing this, Gary's in the nursing home again. He's dying. We thought it was going to happen two weeks ago. It could be today or tomorrow or next week. Who knows?

One evening when I was over there, I could hardly hear him. As I got my ear right up to his lips, he said, "Just treat me like one of your students."

It broke my heart.

I said, "Gary, you're not one of my students. You're my brother." And I took his hand.

It's the same for all of us, I wanted to tell him. We're not that far apart.

10

Ascension Day

Ask, and it shall be given you; seek, and ye shall find; knock, and it shall be opened unto you.

— *Matthew 7:7*

In the spring of 2013 I'd moved from the Liwan to the Antioch Catholic Church, where Father Domenico Bertogli, the white-haired Italian priest who'd coauthored a lovely book about the history of Antioch, rented rooms at reasonable rates to religious pilgrims, tourists, and even the occasional Western journalist like me. My room was perfect, pine-paneled and spare. Though narrow, it had a high ceiling and intricate stone floor; a single bed under a painting of Mary and her child; a metal desk, a lamp, and a chair. Above the desk was an arched window that opened onto the balcony and a view of the courtyard below.

On the first Sunday in June, I was sitting on the balcony and watching doves wheel in a perfect circle above the church, the mosque next door, and the cobbled streets that I had by now come to think of as my neighborhood. The dovecote was on the roof of a three-hundred-year-old stone house. Clouds had moved in from the southwest, and it was starting to rain again. The leaves of the orange and lemon trees in the church courtyard were that new green I loved so much, even more than the deep red of the hibiscus and the yellow of its silly tongue. I wanted to take my morning walk along the river, but I was enjoying the sound of the rain falling on the stones of the courtyard, the red tiles of the roofs, and then rushing down the metal gutters. The sound let up every few moments only to be renewed again, diminished, renewed, like hope itself.

Five hundred miles to the northwest, Istanbul had been racked by the Gezi Park demonstrations, which first began as an environmental protest against an urban development plan for Taksim Gezi Park and then quickly morphed into a massive, nearly revolutionary movement opposed to the government of Recep Tayyip Erdoğan and his crackdown against secularism and the individual rights of free expression and peaceful dissent.

The demonstrations had become nationwide, and the previous night, after dark had fully fallen, the sirens, automobile horns, and muffled booms of tear-gas canisters let me know that Antioch, too, was still roiling with discontent. I took a walk through the neighborhood and saw old women and young mothers banging on pots and pans, even encouraging their toddlers and babies in strollers to do the same, all the while smiling at me to make sure I approved. The border between rich and poor had been breached. There was laughter and music. An unending line of cars wound through the streets with blaring speakers on their roofs. Celebrants wearing Guy Fawkes masks hung out of the windows.

That was the way it was on my side of the river, anyway. On the other side, police and army units had moved in to clear the largely college-age demonstrators, and there a twenty-two-year-old student, Abdullah Cömert, would be fatally injured that night, the second protester to be killed in Turkey during the demonstrations. When I crossed the river and felt the sting of tear gas, I knew I was about to step over a line that I shouldn't, so I returned to the church, listened to the uproar until it died down, and fell into a fitful sleep. There was nothing to fear in Father Domenico's courtyard, and sometimes it also felt like there was nowhere outside it that was safe.

I'd bought a used Marine Kevlar jacket at a militia supply store in Lubbock and brought it with me this time, because I planned on going to Aleppo again. The fighting had only gotten worse since I'd been there in March, but the main threat now to Western journalists was that of kidnapping. On June 6, two French journalists, Didier François and Edouard Elias, had disappeared on the road to Aleppo, and suspicion quickly fell on either al-Nusra or the newer, more fiercely radical ISIS. But there was also, I thought, a window of opportunity. The White House had recently indicated that because of a small but confirmed poison-gas attack by the regime on an Aleppo neighborhood in March, America would finally provide lethal military aid to elements of the Free Syrian Army. According to the reports, this aid would consist only of ammunition and small arms, but the gesture gave hope to the moderate rebels.

That window of opportunity would be brief, though. Bashar al-Assad soon announced a military offensive to retake rebel-held portions of Aleppo and ultimately drive his enemies out of northern Syria altogether. If I was going to go to Aleppo, it would have to be before the launching of Bashar's offensive. Even then, I agonized over the decision I was going to have to make.

The night I learned about the disappearance of the Frenchmen, I had dinner with one of the twenty-five or so families that attended Father Domenico's church. I'd made friends with the three children, especially the oldest boy, Jean-Pierre, who went to college in Gaziantep and also had a job there, and his teenage sister, Elena, a high school senior in Antioch. Both were musicians, spoke English, and were happy to have a native speaker with whom to practice. Their parents were named Jesus and Mary. They spoke no English, but Mary and I knew enough polite Arabic to be able to communicate a little. The best form of communication, though, was simply sitting down at the table in the courtyard of their home and eating the food that Mary had prepared. I couldn't have identified or told you the wonderful things I was consuming at breakneck speed. All I can say is that they were delicious and when I was finished, I was stuffed. I thought the meal had ended.

That's how little I knew about Turkish hospitality. I was aware that Jesus had been hunting in the mountains that afternoon, and before the rest of us sat down to eat, he had brought in his kill, a wild boar slung across his shoulders. He hung it on a hook dangling in front of the door, expertly used a knife to skin it, disembowel it, and cut its flesh into chunks that he threw into an enormous plastic receptacle. It never occurred to me to consider the possibility that he or Mary intended to further cut those chunks into smaller pieces and skewer them for kebabs. After much tea and conversation between me and the two older children, I thought I'd do them a favor by taking them to my favorite café, the Sade Kahve, for dessert.

I wish now I could relive that night. Jean-Pierre returned to Gaziantep, I rarely saw Jesus again, but Mary always smiled and exchanged greetings in Arabic when we saw each other at church or along the alleyways of the neighborhood, and whenever Elena and I crossed paths, she always stopped and told me she was praying for me. This was especially meaningful when she and the other young people from the church would be boarding a bus to go out of town for, say, St. Paul's day, which they would celebrate in Tarsus, or the day of the Blessed Virgin, which they would celebrate at Mary's House outside Ephesus. I can still feel those prayers, at this exact moment, as I'm writing this.

Later in June, on a Saturday, Father Domenico and his parishioners gathered to mark the day of Ascension, that occasion when Jesus bid farewell to his disciples and rose into heaven through a spiral of doves and a column of blinding light. "And, lo, I am with you always," he is reported in the book of Matthew to have said, "even unto the end of the world."

Some scholars believe that this account of the Ascension had been written in Antioch less than a hundred years after the crucifixion, so as I stood on the balcony above the Catholic parishioners, I wondered what it must have been like for Antioch's first-century pagans and Jews when they got word that a man had risen from the dead and ascended into heaven after promising to return again. At that exact moment, and this is no lie, a rainbow lorikeet flew down from the sky and landed in a flurry of wings at the children's feet. It was the loveliest bird I'd ever seen—scarlet, azure, gold, and green.

One of the boys chased the bird under a concrete bench, and then Father Domenico bent down to capture it. When he stood up, he extended his arms, opened his palms, and set the bird free to flutter above the lemon trees before it was taken up and out of sight by a Mediterranean breeze. The scene reminded me of a story from one of the gnostic gospels in which a young Jesus molds a bird out of clay, breathes life into it, and gives it flight.

Something else happened during Mass that evening—a trick of the senses, a suggestion made manifest. I am not a Catholic, so I couldn't partake of the Eucharist, but as Father Domenico passed the silver chalice from the penitent on one side of me to the penitent on the other, I thought I saw a slow, cresting wave in the bowl, thicker and darker than wine could ever be. *Tinto negro,* the Argentinians might call it. Black wine. But it looked like blood to me. It really did.

After Mass an American family introduced themselves. They weren't exactly tourists. The father was a newly appointed federal judge from Detroit, and he and his wife and two of their children, a son and a daughter, had come to Antioch to accompany their older daughter back to America after her year of teaching in Turkey. They invited me to join them for dinner at the Leban, and as we walked there, I asked the girl privately if she'd told her parents about those twin car bombings in Reyhanlı that had killed more than fifty people just a month before. She shook her head; she hadn't wanted to worry them. But I insisted she tell them, because I wanted them to know how courageous she had been to teach in this volatile region. As was true of even very well informed Americans, her parents hadn't heard about the bombings until then.

In Antioch, the bombings were considered the single greatest horror of the war so far, a tragedy that had occurred on Turkish soil, very close to them. The Turkish government had placed the guilt on Bashar's security apparatus and had arrested a Turk who confessed his complicity. Not everyone was convinced, though. Some thought

a radical Islamist group might have been the culprit. I was just glad
I'd been able to go back to Reyhanlı to see that Aini was okay.

After dinner I left to nurse my nightly Efes, a Turkish bottled beer,
at the rooftop restaurant called Asia, where I customarily watched
the mad ballet of the swallows, the moonrise over Mount Silpius,
and the lights coming on in the streets and on the rooftops of the
Arabic quarter that climbed its flanks. I sat at a table with a BBC
television crew. They hadn't gone into Syria and didn't intend to, but
their security man had been there. He'd also been to Iraq, in particular to a police station in the southern town of Majar al-Kabir, where
six British military police had been murdered by a mob in 2003.
"The blood," he said. "I couldn't believe how much blood there was."

I asked him whether it was a good idea to take my Kevlar jacket
to Aleppo. He said of course it was a good idea, but when I asked if I
should buy a helmet at one of the military surplus stores, he said no,
because the only people who wore helmets in this war were Bashar's
troops, and I might be mistaken for one of them. Then we traded
stories about the worst assignments we'd ever had to cover back
home. One of the BBC guys said he'd been called to the scene of a
suicide in which the man had stepped in front of a train, and the
ambulance drivers were having trouble removing the body because
its halves were held together by a length of flesh so pressed upon the
rail that they had to use an axe to chop it in two. The others of us
decided on less tragic fare: alien spacecraft, cockroach infestations,
and dogs who could, or would not, talk.

But then silence fell, and I got up to go.

"I don't want to die," I told them.

No one smiled. They just stood, shook my hand, and gave me the
customary "Be safe."

Two days later I took the 6:20 a.m. dolmuş to Kilis. The van was
packed. The woman seated next to me had two daughters in her lap.
One of them was sick and vomited as we wound up into the moun-

tains. By 9:00 a.m., when I got to the Hotel Istanbul in Kilis, there were no available rooms, but two Germans, a photographer and a print journalist, were just finishing packing up their equipment in the lobby. They'd come well prepared, with helmets, flak jackets, food, water, and medical kits. When they were ready to go, we shared a cab to the Turkish border crossing and hitched a ride to the other side.

The Syrian men there crowded around, asking for cigarettes and pumping us for information about where we were going and why. My driver didn't come a minute too soon.

"Did you hear about the French guys?" the print reporter whispered before I climbed into the van.

I nodded, and we parted with the usual "Be safe."

Clean-shaven Anas was at the main office in Azaz. When I walked in, he introduced me to a roomful of village elders wearing kaftans and keffiyehs, each of whom greeted me with an embrace and a kiss on each cheek. Anas said they wanted to thank me for America's promise of weapons for the FSA. When we were out of earshot, though, he told me that none of the aid had arrived yet.

"I guess you heard about the French journalists," he said. I told him I had.

He denied a rumor that fighters from al-Nusra or ISIS were present in Azaz, but he said he couldn't speak with confidence about the road to Aleppo. "That's why Wahid's your driver this time."

I glanced back at the man who'd driven me from the border. He was leaning against the silver van, thick arms akimbo. He looked like a pro wrestler or animal trainer, and when he opened the van door, he smiled a thin, elliptical smile. "So you want to go to Aleppo?"

I shrugged and told him to take me to whatever he thought I ought to see.

In that case, he said, we'd have to be accompanied by someone armed. First, though, we had to stop by his house for bottled water.

Wahid and his wife lived on a sandy street of whitewashed stone houses. Her name meant "the eyes of a wild beast." They had five children—four daughters and a seven-year-old son. Wahid claimed their town was bombed and strafed almost every night. "This morning I woke up to a huge blast," he said.

When I asked where his family hid, he said there was nowhere to hide. They just lay there and tried to go back to sleep. "The children and I do, anyway. My wife still has a hard time."

I suggested the obvious, that they ought to leave Azaz.

"And go where?" He said they'd be killed if they headed south into regime-held territory.

"What about Turkey?" He said no one in his family had passports and reminded me that the border was closed to undocumented refugees because of overcrowding in the camps on the Turkish side. He added that the closest refugee camp on the Syrian side was no safer than Azaz. It, too, had been bombed, that muddy sinkhole of disease, where more than ten thousand people lived in plastic tents.

"Better to stay here." He pointed to the mosque that had suffered a direct hit from one of Assad's warplanes. Alongside it in the pile of rubble was a crushed sedan and a fire-ravaged armored personnel carrier.

"This is our home," he said.

The armed fighter that Wahid picked up on the outskirts of Azaz was named Nasir. Bald and full-bearded, he appeared even more solidly built than Wahid, and he carried his AK-47 effortlessly, as if to emphasize that point. While he made himself comfortable in one of the rear seats, I took my Kevlar jacket out of my backpack and laid it on the floor behind me. I'd never worn one before, and this one had a bullet hole in the back. Wahid smiled when he saw it, so I told him to let me know if we got to a place where he thought I might need to put it on.

He agreed to do that, and then he told me the regime was using "vacuum bombs," a kind of thermobaric weapon that had been employed by the United States in Vietnam, by the Russians in Afghanistan and Chechnya, and, according to the FSA, by Bashar al-Assad's forces in the

Battle of Aleppo. Wahid claimed that the vacuum created was powerful enough to suck the brains out of the enemy. He said he'd seen the dead men before burial, some of them friends of his. Except for the flap of loose skull at the back of their heads, they looked like they were still alive. But there was nothing at all inside their heads.

He pointed out remains of recently bombed houses and shops. Some were already in the process of being rebuilt. "They bomb at night," he said. "We rebuild in the morning."

I remembered the article about what had happened in Azaz in January, when twenty-five people had been killed in a daylight bombing raid as they queued up in line for bread.

"What else can we do?" Wahid said. "We've got to eat." And four miles south of town, he pointed out the control tower at Menagh, the government air base used by Assad's regime to launch warplane and helicopter attacks on Azaz and other towns in the region. Four of Wahid's brothers, his natural ones, not just comrades or friends, were among the rebels fighting at Menagh at that very minute, and he said he joined them whenever he was asked. "It's going to fall," he said. "God willing, it'll fall tonight."

He smiled and said that prisoners of war wouldn't be an issue then. "Whenever we find somebody who supports the regime, our God tells us we can kill them. So we do."

Then he told me it was time to remove the battery from my cell phone. Bashar's army used cell signals to pinpoint targets, he said, and a line of cars on our rural two-lane, even funerals or wedding parties, could be bombed by government planes at any moment. It had happened many times, most recently a week before. The bride and her father had been among the dead.

"What about three guys in a silver minivan?" I asked. "Do you think Bashar would bomb them?"

For the first time, Wahid didn't smile. "This is nothing to joke about," he said.

So I removed my cell battery and stared straight ahead as the landscape of northern Syria unrolled like a banquet table gone to rot—burnt fields, piles of rank garbage, and emaciated dogs lying in the dirt. In the blasted villages I saw jerry-rigged antiaircraft guns tilted in the beds of smoldering pickups, and groups of rebel fighters, including two preteens on a moped, the boy in back armed with a Kalashnikov.

In one village we passed a garage where Wahid said rebels were manufacturing their own weapons. A group of men appeared to be mounting a heavy machine gun on a truck, but we didn't stop. America and Europe had deserted them, Wahid said, and the Western TV crew who'd recently wanted to video the manufacturing process had been told to scram or face the consequences, which wouldn't, Wahid said, have been good.

Between villages, there were only a few vehicles on the road other than our own. We must have passed through nearly a dozen checkpoints, each manned by thin rebel fighters under the black flag of al-Nusra. Occasionally we'd also see one belonging to ISIS, which differed from al-Qaeda's only in the addition of a large circle with lettering inside, a crude duplication of the Prophet's official seal.

"Don't worry," Wahid said. "Most of them know who I am."

I was not much reassured by that. Almost all the flags I'd seen in March had been those of the Free Syrian Army. But since that last visit to Aleppo, unlikely alliances were being made between the various rebel groups.

Wahid said he wanted to take me to meet Abdulkader al-Saleh, who went by the pseudonym Hajji Marea and was the leader of the military wing of Al Tawhid, the largest group of rebel fighters in Aleppo. Wahid said Hajji Marea was someone who could work with President Obama, as though I had connections to the president. I pretended I didn't know who Hajji Marea was, and of course I didn't mention that I'd recently read he was cooperating with al-Nusra. I simply declined Wahid's invitation.

The black flags were not a good sign.

Wahid slowed when we passed the entrance to Bashar's former military academy and at the checkpoint a little farther on where a road led to the province's largest prison. The seizure of the military academy had been one of the first rebel victories in the war, but the prison was still being held by government soldiers even though it had been surrounded by rebels for months.

"Those guys are crazy," Wahid said of the soldiers. "One time, because they wouldn't surrender, we rounded up ten of their supporters, shot them, and hung them on the courtyard gate."

When he turned back to me, he was smiling. "Even then, they wouldn't surrender. So we bulldozed the gate, drove a truck inside, and dumped many more bodies in the courtyard where they could see them."

I asked him what the soldiers did then.

"They started shooting prisoners in the head one by one and throwing them out the upper windows, so we decided to pull back. Now we're just waiting for them to starve." He smiled again, and that's when Aleppo loomed ahead of us under smoke from fields of burning wheat.

The city was exactly as I remembered it from March—the same collapsed apartment buildings, only more of them; the same neighborhoods flattened by Scuds or barrel bombs; the same buses stacked on top of one another to stop sniper bullets, only now the stacks of buses were three high instead of two, and in the gaps between the stacks stood walls of dirt higher than a man's head. The most striking difference, though, was the presence of automobile traffic and unarmed civilians on the streets. There were even vegetable vendors on the stretch in front of the bombed-out Dar al-Shifa Hospital, and a clandestine clinic that had taken the same name as the hospital had opened up on a side street.

"Everybody's stocking up for the regime offensive," Wahid said.

I asked him when he thought it might start.

"It started yesterday, with tanks and Hezbollah fighters, but we stopped them. Hezbollah is so weak, they ran away. Their big bad image has just been created by the Western media."

In the clinic, a thirty-year-old doctor in a Beatles T-shirt was in a curtained-off alcove near the front door. The curtain was opened a bit. He was removing a bullet from a patient's leg, so we did what visitors to any clinic or hospital in America might do: we sat in the waiting room and watched TV. The only difference was that this TV was tuned to Aleppo Today, an underground station that produced a constant stream of videos about the conflict, including scenes of the early protest movement followed by revolutionary music, the rise of the armed opposition, and then a deluge of explosions, scenes of regime planes being shot down and children being rescued from bombed apartment buildings. All of this was interspersed with Aleppo's version of weather reports, except that these reports were about which neighborhoods to avoid that day, the location of snipers, and lists of the day's dead.

A man with a terribly blackened foot and lower leg politely interrupted our viewing, but we explained that the doctor was with another patient, and behind all this music and commentary from the TV screen, I heard what sounded like the scream of a very real child down the clinic's hallway.

When the doctor appeared, toweling off his hands, he sent the man to another alcove and pulled that curtain closed before he sat on the arm of a chair and talked to us. He said he'd been at the hospital the day it had been bombed. Among the more than forty dead were two children and a nurse, but the injuries he saw now were different. Most were the result of gunshots to the abdomen or chest, wounds that had been caused by snipers. Fewer casualties were from shelling or mortars, none from chemicals yet — and he estimated the breakdown at forty percent children, twenty percent women, the rest of them men, some fighters, some not. The doctor said he worked mornings in the rebel-held side of the city and afternoons at a hospital in the regime-held side. Nobody knew he was doing this, but it was normal for him, despite the fact that he had a wife and baby on the rebel side and hated the Assad regime. He was a doctor, he said. He took care of the injured.

When I asked whether he was optimistic now that America had promised more aid, he said he hadn't seen any of it yet, and then he told me what I'd heard from almost every Syrian I'd met in the opposition: "We don't trust promises. We need something we can touch."

My own problem was that I didn't know what I needed. I'd heard the stories at refugee camps of husbands and sons being spirited away by armed men to certain death, of neighbors lined up and executed in broad daylight. I'd witnessed the suffering of the children at that hospital in Reyhanlı, along with their strength and courage. And in Aleppo I'd watched men search through the rubble for the remains of their wives and children. I'd had to run for cover with my driver and translator when the explosions got too close. What more did I need or want?

I just didn't know. All I knew was that there had been reports of fierce street fighting in the alleyways of the Old City, so when Wahid suggested we head there, I said of course we should go.

Wahid thought someone he knew, a member of the regime's security apparatus who had defected to the Free Syrian Army, might let us pass through the gate that he and his men guarded. So we parked at one of ancient Aleppo's seven entrances, this one called the Gate to the Grave, where Wahid pointed out his friend standing erect in a shaft of brilliant sunlight. His khakis were pressed; his hair was glistening and perfectly in place. In one hand he held a half-eaten falafel wrapped in pita bread, in the other, a grenade.

The flags flying above and around the man unnerved me. The Arabic script on the flags was the commonplace *shahada,* the Islamic declaration of faith: "There is no God but God. His name is Allah, and Muhammad is his messenger." But black meant that the flags belonged to al-Nusra, suggesting that to fly any other flag might invite an unhappy response.

In addition to shooting a Syrian child to death for allegedly dishonoring the name of Allah and executing a Syrian woman because she had been accused of adultery, al-Nusra also had a nasty history of kidnapping foreigners, in particular Theo Padnos, an American a writer who disappeared one day from Antioch, having been lured just across the border into Syria by al-Nusra operatives, and was then beaten, tortured, and held prisoner in unspeakable conditions for nearly two years. Of course, I didn't know about that kidnapping yet. It was enough for me that al-Nusra was al-Qaeda, pure and simple, the same al-Qaeda that had killed nearly three thousand Americans on 9/11.

After some thought, Wahid's friend at the Gate to the Grave said he'd give us permission to pass, but he insisted we first have tea with him. So we sat on wooden benches in the sunlight while we did that, and his sons—ages seven or eight and dressed in child-size fatigues—begged to hold the AK-47s that leaned against the wall, a request their father refused. One of the boys wanted me to see the toe of his tennis shoe, to which a photograph of President Assad had been stitched, the ultimate insult in Islamic culture. There was no question what this boy would be doing in a few years—that is, if he were still alive.

When we finally waved goodbye to Wahid's friend and his sons, we drove through the Gate to the Grave under an enormous banner in Arabic that urged the residents of Aleppo to be patient in their troubles. Allah would provide. At first the narrow street into the Old City was filled with shoppers, as though there were no war. But the variety of goods appeared slim. We passed wooden booths stacked with used clothes, cigarette cartons, and bottles of benzene for use in Molotov cocktails, but nothing was as disheartening as what came next, the ancient Al-Madina Souq, the world-famous Aleppo covered market. Here the street branched into alleyways, the booths and their meager wares disappeared, and the dark closed in around us except for the glint of our headlights on the bullet-pocked walls, the fire-blackened ceiling, and the distant barrels of guns. A group of rebels emerged slowly out of the dark like photographic prints from a stop bath. They were rough-cut, lean, and covered in dust, and their eyes, although fixed on us through the windshield, didn't appear to see us at all.

When they ordered us to stop, we got out of the van, and the discussion that began politely enough turned into something of a debate. I thought the fighters were gesturing in my direction, but Nasir lifted his weapon to his waist and the men calmed down a bit. Then he and Wahid walked slowly back to the van.

"Is there a problem?" I asked.

"I don't know," Wahid said. All he knew was that we had to turn back, and I didn't mind that at all. It felt good to be leaving the shrouded, dank wreck that had once been the jewel of Aleppo; it felt good to reenter the light.

At the entrance to the Old City again, I didn't get out of the van. Wahid and Nasir did, and Nasir ended up staying at the guard post. When Wahid came back to the van, the captain of the guard was with him. The captain insisted he go back with us to the dark spot in the burned-out market where we'd been stopped by the other rebels. He said he would take care of them. Once again we wound through those narrow, blackened alleyways, and Wahid said that up ahead was a shrine where tradition had it that Zechariah, the father of John the Baptist, had been buried. It surprised me that Zechariah had been a figure in both the Quran and the Bible. I didn't fully realize how closely the texts mirrored each other until then.

This time the rebel fighters were willing to let us pass, so we left the van with them and went the rest of the way on foot. Before long, Wahid said we had entered the Great Mosque, which was still being fought over, he added, by both sides. I asked him whether I ought to go back for my Kevlar jacket. He said no, and since neither he nor his friend were wearing such gear, I didn't insist.

The Great Mosque of Aleppo had been one of the most favored destinations for pilgrims from the Muslim world and beyond. Some thought it lovelier than the larger Great Mosque of Damascus, which was a little older (construction in Aleppo started in 715, around the same year the mosque in Damascus opened), and the one in Damascus supposedly contained something more treasured than the remains of John the Baptist's father: the head of John the Baptist himself.

There's no way to describe the size and splendor of the Great Mosque of Aleppo as it appears in photos before the war. I won't attempt it here. The desolation is easier to convey: Leningrad, 1942. A piece of it, anyway. The first stop we made seemed to be a forward command post, with battle-weary fighters and bored clerks. The scar-faced fighter who first approached us wore a camouflage vest but otherwise looked like he'd just completed a roller derby match. He had on a brilliant blue shirt and white tennis shoes. I'd later find out he wore blue because it was the color in Islam most associated with protection, and Wahid told me the mirror hanging from his belt was what he used to look around corners for snipers. But not even Wahid could account for the extraordinary whiteness of the man's shoes.

The fighter in blue stepped closer, and after the elaborate customary greetings in Arabic, he tried out his English on me: "Obama is good," he said. "Bashar is bad. America is good. Russia is bad." What I heard him say next was that he missed Iraq. He missed fighting with the Americans, but mostly he missed their whiskey, and after he said all of this, Wahid touched my elbow and whispered, "It's just a joke. Understand?" It was then I noticed the black patches, like miniature al-Nusra or ISIS flags, on the fighter in blue's vest.

"We both have books," he said. "You have your Bible. We have our Quran. But we worship the same God."

The fighter motioned to a couple of the other men, who were armed with AK-47s, and then strapped a pearl-handled pistol to his chest. "Come with me," he said.

I glanced at Wahid. He indicated yes, so I followed the fighter in blue down a long, dark corridor filled with rubble. One of the other men led the way. Wahid and another fighter brought up the rear. There was sunlight and air at the end of the corridor, where it opened into an arcade along the enormous courtyard of the mosque — a safe place, I thought — but everyone stopped before we got to the sunlight. The first man in line glanced back at the fighter in blue before bending over and running through the sunlight, across the debris, and into the darkness of a large room on the other side.

I felt a hand on my back. It belonged to the fighter in blue. "When I tell you, duck low and run."

He paused, and then said: "Go!"

That's what I did, as did he and the others. The distant sound of four evenly spaced gunshots, like hammer on steel, followed us into the dark room on the other side.

What they had wanted to show me in this room, heavily fortified with stone blocks and sandbags, was a view over the bags to the mosque's enormous courtyard, a wasteland of broken masonry, tile, and metal scaffolding fallen on its side. The hat-shaped ablution fountains in the middle of the courtyard were bullet-riddled, and the enormous pile of rubble in the far corner was where the mosque's minaret, five stories high and fourteen hundred years old, had once stood. The rebels said it had been blown to pieces by a regime tank, but the Syrian government had blamed the destruction on them. A photograph of the courtyard and minaret as they had looked before the war was pasted on the wall beside that view, and underneath the photograph were what appeared to be bloodstains.

It was in this somber setting in the Great Mosque of Aleppo that one of the men used bottled gas and a Bunsen burner to brew us a cup of tea. In a place like this, there is a silence that accompanies otherwise routine pleasantries. They take on enormous significance — a cup of tea, a cigarette, or even a pair of new white shoes. This silence has to do with faith and its ability, no matter what the circumstances, to keep the mind and spirit focused on peace, without which survival and the future are impossible.

I'm reminded of a story I heard from a resident of Douma, a suburb of Damascus where the street fighting was often brutal and close. Ordinary fighters on both sides, unknown to their top commanders, had worked out a plan so that each man could attend to his familial obligations. The two sides had scheduled their fighting so it would occur only during certain fixed hours of the day or night. The rest of the time, combatants on both sides could go about the routines they'd established prior to the war, procuring food, water, and kerosene for their wives and children, tending any gardens they'd been able to establish on vacant lots as yet untouched by the fighting, or going to their mosques for prayer.

They might pass each other on the street as they went about these peaceful pursuits. But by the time the appointed hours for fighting arrived, they would have returned to their units, taken their positions behind the barricades, and entered combat with the same ferocity as before.

In Aleppo, the only ceasefires I'd heard of were to clear decaying corpses from the streets. It would have been suicide to step into the courtyard of the Great Mosque, but at least what I could do now was partake of the tea, and thank the men who had given it to me.

Afterward I told Wahid I wanted to check out a nave that had been destroyed by tank fire, but he said it smelled too bad. I pulled my shirt up over my mouth and nose, but the odor was too strong; it was the same thing I'd smelled more than twenty years before in the ruins of a Salvadoran neighborhood leveled by thousand-pound bombs: rotting flesh — concussive, like the slamming of a door. So the fighter in blue showed me the opposite arcade instead. He said it had been used by women on their way to prayer — a beautiful space, he said, before the Syrian Army and Hezbollah sacked it.

"Go on. Take a closer look."

I stepped around the stone barricade the rebels used for cover. The ordnance impacts indicated a ferocious battle had taken place there. The walls and ceiling were spangled by bullets, like stars in an unholy universe. It was hard to imagine what that arcade must have looked like before the war, although I'd later see it in photographs. But I wanted to see more of it now, so I took a few steps farther until another of the fighters, older and in starched fatigues, grabbed me by the shoulder and said, "No. There are snipers here, too."

The problem now was getting back to the place where we'd first met the men. We'd have to retrace the way we'd come. And it was damned if you did, damned if you didn't, like spies, like religion, like my brother and me.

When we reached the sunlit arcade where we'd run under sniper fire, I felt a hand on my back again.

"This time," the fighter in blue said, "duck lower. Run faster." And he ran beside me the whole way, his hand pressed hard against my shoulder blade.

There were no gunshots this time. But at the end of the arcade, he said he wanted me to see one more thing: a crude wooden ladder, about fourteen feet high, that led to a hole in the wall below a domed ceiling. The hole looked like the entry or exit point of a rocket-propelled grenade round. When I asked why the ladder was there, he told me the fighting had been so intense in the mosque that the ladder had been the only way he and his friends could remove their dead.

I looked at that hole high up on the wall and tried to imagine how anyone could have done that, carry dead men one by one up a ladder in the middle of a war.

"Here," he said, and he directed my attention to the lower rungs. "See the blood?"

The rungs appeared to be covered with it. I'm not a forensic scientist, but I'd seen plenty of blood before in El Salvador, and in the gutters after automobile accidents, and while my daughters were being born. This looked like blood to me, and given the circumstances in which I saw it, the expertise of the witness who identified it, and the logic that surrounded the events that had clearly taken place in the Great Mosque of Aleppo, I concluded that this was blood on the rungs of a ladder that led to the Gate to the Grave.

I was in an Islamic mosque, on the heels of the Christian day of Ascension, at an intersection where the three major monotheistic religions met. Jacob had been the father of the tribes of Israel, and here there was blood on the bottom rungs of a ladder like the one Jacob had seen in a dream, although this ladder was made of wood instead of gold. No angels had been walking up it, only Muslim brothers carrying the bodies of their dead friends. They had taken them to an upper room like the one in which an insurrectionist named Jesus and his followers had celebrated the Passover by sharing a supper accompanied by wine that he had turned into blood. And the Passover itself had commemorated that moment in history when blood marked the doorways of Jewish homes so that the children inside would not be killed.

The God of the three great religions was as invisible as air, but here he was enshrined in the middle of a mosque, in the middle of a war. Yes, it was Jacob's ladder, the one we Christian children used to sing that we were climbing as "soldiers of the Cross." It was also the ladder the Ottomans had mounted to breach the walls of Byzantium.

I'd found the evidence of things not seen, that part of faith that belief is made of, but I hadn't yet found the substance of things hoped for. Here in this profoundly holy religious place, the only substance I'd found was blood.

In the Apostles' Creed that my parents and I had affirmed every Sunday, one critical line had been left out. After the words "Jesus suffered under Pontius Pilate and was crucified, dead, and buried," and before the line about ascending into heaven, the original Apostles' Creed was supposed to say "He descended into Hell."

Perhaps that's why I'd always found him in war. As the Psalmist said, "if I make my bed in hell, behold, thou art there."

We left the mosque by the same route we'd come in, and at the blackened ruins where we'd left the van, we gave a lift to a young archaeology student who worked as a medic in the morning and then tried to rescue antiquities from the mosque in the afternoon. The rebels wouldn't let him do it that day, though. It was too dangerous, they said, and as we passed back through the Gate to the Grave, there was a huge explosion. It was the loudest blast I'd ever heard— but I felt it more than I heard it. The people in the street hardly took notice, and I continued to interview the archaeology student until he said he had to go. But I knew then that I'd been injured internally, and I wrote two words in the margin next to the interview: *vacuum bomb?*

Coming out of Aleppo, Wahid took a torturous route through the side streets, and the road back to Azaz was not the same road we'd taken that morning. It was overgrown with weeds and empty of vehicles or any other sign of life. "We never come back the same way we came," he explained.

11

The Absence of Fear

I knew even before I left Syria that I'd suffered some kind of internal head injury. I supposed it had been the result of that loud blast on our way out of the Old City, though no one else seemed to have been affected by it. I didn't say anything to Wahid, and I kept interviewing the archaeology student. But I knew. Nothing like that had ever happened to me before.

Wahid and I hardly spoke on the way back to the border. He let me off on the Syrian side, near the tent camp where children had died the previous winter when their kerosene stoves set the plastic tents on fire. There were no border formalities. I walked the mile to the Turkish side but didn't see anybody to stamp my passport on reentry. I didn't know where they were, and I didn't look for them. I didn't care. There was a single taxi in the parking lot, but I didn't know where to tell him to take me.

He asked where I'd come from. I said Aleppo, but that I didn't want to go back there. He said he couldn't take me even if I did. "Where did you come from before Syria?"

I said Antioch.

He told me the last bus to Antioch had already left.

"Then you take me," I said.

"It's a long way," he said, "and expensive."

I tried to think of alternatives, but couldn't.

"I don't care what it costs," I said. "Just take me to Antioch."

As we came down off the high plateau from Kilis, the sun was low above range after range of the highest mountains I'd ever seen, but there was still enough light to illuminate the vineyards being blown around by the wind, each vine waving its tendrils and leaves as though to welcome me home. I wanted to write that in my notebook but fell asleep, and when I woke up a couple of hours later, it was dark, and we'd pulled over on the shoulder at the interchange where one highway led to Hatay Airport and the other into the city.

The taxi driver had been waiting for me to wake up. He said he had to call another driver to take me into the city itself. He wasn't licensed to do that.

I told him I needed to go to the Catholic Church. He didn't know where or what a Catholic Church was, but the driver he was calling would.

The new one didn't know where the church was, either, but I must have been able to stop him on the old Roman Road at the mosque in front of the church. I don't remember getting out of the cab, walking up the stairs to my room, or lying down and falling back asleep. What I do recall is waking up fully clothed, late in the afternoon the next day, and remembering that I had a dinner engagement with a new friend I'd made on my last flight from Istanbul to Antioch on what was by then being called "the Jihadi Express."

Her name was Hazan. She had been sitting in a forward section filled with what appeared to be Chinese or Chechen fighters. They made her nervous, so she asked the stewardess to move her toward the rear, where there was an empty seat next to mine. She'd been an exchange student in America and had gotten her graduate degree there, so her English was perfect. She was now a professor, and she was returning from an academic conference in Vienna. She was unhappy at her university, where the chief administrative positions were staffed according to the Sunni hierarchy. The imams ran the university, she said, in the same way they ran the country.

Hazan was already seated at a table near the back of the Anadolu Restaurant, under a date palm tree whose trunk had been wound about with a string of tiny white lights.

"So," she said, "did you go to Aleppo?"

I nodded.

"How was it?"

"Something broke inside my head."

She smiled at me, delighted. "I bet it did!" she said.

"No, seriously, something broke in my head."

"What do you mean?"

"I don't know."

She was still smiling broadly, a lovely smile that charmed even the most tight-assed headwaiters. "Was it something you felt?"

"Yes."

"Well, what was it like?"

"It was like something broke inside my head."

Now we both had to laugh, because there was no way for us to bridge this impasse. When we stopped, though, she said, "Is it painful?"

I shook my head. "It's more complicated than that."

"Okay. I think I understand. What are you going to order?"

"I don't know. Do you mind ordering for me?"

"All right, but you have got to work on your Turkish, Dennis, and this menu even has English subtitles, so there's no excuse."

Back in Texas, Gary needed an assisted living facility. He hated the nursing home and he was refusing to go to his physical therapy sessions. Assisted living was a risk, but we were running out of money so I felt I had to get home, to honor his request.

I was beginning to think that I needed assisted living myself. Because I had failed to have my passport stamped when I reentered Turkey after going to Aleppo, passport control at the Istanbul airport wouldn't let me board my plane back to the States. They claimed I was in Turkey illegally, and they took me to the police for questioning. It didn't help when I told the officers that I'd been into Syria and that the border must have been closed when I got out. The questions centered on exactly what I was doing in Syria, and the fact that I was a writer didn't make things easier. As I'd been told before, Turkey had more writers in prison than any other country in Europe.

The police didn't seem interested in another mouth to feed in prison, though, so I would just have to pay a 2,000 Turkish lira fine ($1,000 US), and I wouldn't be allowed back into Turkey for three years. The fine, although very steep, was not the worst part of the penalty. I *had* to be able to come back to Turkey, so I asked if there was anything I could do for them that might make it possible for me to return sooner to their lovely country. The policeman behind the desk asked if I meant a bribe. Of course not, I said, and smiled as though the thought hadn't occurred to me until that very moment. The policeman did not smile. He just pointed with his pen to a camera mounted on the wall above him.

"Is there *any*thing I can do?" I said, this time in desperation.

But now it was the policeman's turn to smile. "Well, you can always go back to the border and ask them to stamp your passport."

"Three weeks after the fact?"

"That would be illegal on their part," he said, "but you could try." The son of a bitch was enjoying this. "Would you like to pay your fine now?"

I shook my head. I did not pay the fine.

So this was how I had wound up in Gaziantep, the closest airport to the border crossing at Kilis. I found a room at a hotel that Henri had once suggested. From there, I called Henri and explained the problem. He said he could drive up to Gaziantep and take me to the border, but that it would be very expensive and that there was no guarantee of success. The only previous experience he'd had with something like this was when a British photographer had been caught reentering Turkey under the barbed wire at Yayladağı, and Henri had gone to court with him as a translator. The judge lowered the fine but confiscated the man's camera equipment, and still barred him from entering the country for three years.

I'd come this far, though, and I didn't have any camera equipment. It was worth a try.

Henri put on what must have been the performance of his life in front of those Turkish border authorities. He said that I was writing a beautiful book about Turkey and its people, and he listed some of the actors and actresses who would star in the film adaptation, including the young Turkish actress whose photograph was pinned on the bulletin board behind the chief official's desk. Henri even reenacted a scene from the book, a comic scene that sent the men bouncing on their heels in delight. The chief pounded his desk. "No, no!" he kept saying. And then he turned to me and in a very serious voice said, "There is one thing you must do."

"What's he saying?" I asked Henri.

"He says he wants you to send him an autographed copy when the book comes out."

"Oh yes. Tell him I'd be delighted to."

Thus was my passport stamped and my return to Turkey assured.

Ten days later ISIS kidnapped two more French journalists, Nicolas Henin and Pierre Torres. A month later they kidnapped American journalist Steven Sotloff only four kilometers south of Azaz, on the same road to Aleppo that Wahid and I had taken, and the day after that, they kidnapped Kayla Mueller, the American humanitarian aid worker, in the center of Aleppo itself.

But I didn't know any of this yet. The kidnappers had told their victims they'd be killed if their names became public. And I was back in Texas sorting out my own domestic and psychological difficulties.

I had concluded that the absence of fear was the most frightening thing in the world. That's why I started seeing a therapist. She was tiny, so tiny she had to tuck her legs under herself in the swiveling office chair. She wore long dresses, hippie style, which she folded beneath her as though they were sheets and she were making a bed, and when she wore skirts that were short, she modestly tugged at the hems to cover her knees.

I was there, I told her, because I was in the throes of a spiritual crisis.

"In what way?"

"I'm not interested in eternal life. When I die, I want to stay dead. In fact, I'm not interested in life at all."

"Have you thought about how you'd do it?"

I said yes, that I wanted to put a bullet through my brother's head and then a bullet through my own. I'd have called the police first. They'd find us on a plastic sheet in the back yard, so there wouldn't be a mess.

"Have you thought things like this before?"

I told her yes, that I had spent three weeks on a psych ward for suicidal ideation more than twenty years before, and another, shorter visit after that for an intentional overdose. "I just did it to get attention," I said, "but all I got was a tube down my throat in the emergency room. When the resident psychiatrist released me the next day, he wrote a prescription for twice as many of the pills I'd taken in the first place."

"Do you have access to a gun?"

"No."

"Do you feel like you need to go to the hospital now?"

"No."

"Okay. So tell me what led you to this spiritual crisis?"

I told her it began at the foot of a ladder in an Islamic mosque in Aleppo, Syria, and that as I was getting out of the old part of the city, something broke inside my head.

"Syria? I understand they're having problems over there."

I told her she was right about that, and like the good therapist she was, she started paying close attention to the news and wanted to talk with me about what she'd learned. Talk about it, not just listen. Most of the psychiatrists I'd dealt with in the past didn't want to do either. I figured I was just an open cash register drawer to them, but I shouldn't complain. I understand many of them have psychological problems of their own, and hey, I get money for pretending to teach students how to write novels and stuff like that.

The assisted living facility I found for Gary was one of the least expensive in the Lubbock area and in many ways the best. All the units were on the ground level in three buildings that formed a horseshoe around a huge green space. Gary's unit was large and high-ceilinged. It had two bedrooms, one of which was for his roommate, and a large kitchenette with all the necessary appliances. A laundromat was down the hall, as was the dispensary for medications. The building's common living area and kitchen were enormous. There was a large-screen TV and built-in bookcases, comfortable furniture, and a caring staff.

In time, Gary would come to hate that place, too. But he could walk to a Subway, Family Dollar store, and park. Those were treasured outings for him. The staff would tell me he walked hours a day. And I took him wherever else he wanted to go, just as I had when he was in the nursing home, but I started drawing the same clear line for him. The minute he started telling me how much he hated Mom, Dad, Scotty, Jeanie, and me for sending him to the state hospital more than fifty years ago, or accusing us of stealing all his money, I would take him back to his room at assisted living. I tried to explain to him that I had my own problems. They were of no interest to him.

Until I headed back to Antioch toward the end of September, I saw my therapist every week except when I was in Birmingham. I went twice, the first time for a family get-together. I drove to the reunion in my older daughter's van, with her and her husband and their three kids in tow. My younger daughter and her husband weren't able to go. When we got to Birmingham, I realized how much the Covington family had shrunk. My father had been one of twelve children. All of them were long dead, as were my mom and dad, my sister, Jeanie, and my older brother Scotty. Only Gary was still alive, and he was in no condition to travel.

The people in attendance at the reunion picnic, which was held in a neighborhood park, were my nephew, Scotty's son; his wife; and their children and grandchildren. We had a nice visit, but my daughter told me later that she could tell something had changed. She had almost made me stop the van on the interstate because she felt I wasn't able to concentrate on the road. She began to wonder if I even knew where I was half the time, and when we got to the reunion and exchanged all the names of the children, I couldn't get them right even when I was looking at the page where I'd just written them down.

"It's Syria, isn't it, Dad?" she asked when we got back to Texas. But she told her mother, Vicki, that she suspected I had the beginnings of dementia.

The next week, on September 14, I took a plane back to Birmingham for the fiftieth anniversary of the bombing of the 16th Street Baptist Church. In some ways the events of that weekend in 1963 seemed closer to me in time than anything since—the stabbing of Connie Bieker on the band bus as we headed to the Friday night football game, and then that Sunday morning two days later, when we came home from church and my father turned the knob of the brown radio that sat on the counter between the stove and the kitchen table, and we learned that a bomb had gone off at the black church downtown and that four girls had been killed.

My idea for this latest visit to my hometown was to stay at my usual lodging, a cheap motel that often served as a place for drug dealers and prostitutes to ply their trades. I intended to interview some of these businesspeople, the black ones anyway, to find out whether Dr. King's dream had been realized and how in retrospect their lives might have been affected or changed by that terrible event on September 15, 1963. Unfortunately, I didn't find any of those folks this time—it wasn't such a good idea anyway—so I resigned myself to the official memorial service at the church.

I expected thousands in the streets. There weren't. Posters, flyers, and newspaper articles had said that shuttle buses would transport people to the church from the parking lot at Legion Field, Birmingham's nearby football stadium, but there were plenty of parking places around the church. My friend Jim Neel, his son Colin, and I found one right across the street. I thought all the church bells in the city would toll at the exact moment, 10:22 a.m., when the bomb had gone off. The only bell I would hear would be the one at the church.

Reporters claimed the church was packed during the service. Not really. I was in the balcony, and there were quite a number of empty seats there. But the sermon Rev. Arthur Price delivered, a combination of the Sunday school lesson that had been used on the very day of the bombing, along with a few contemporary references, was attended to with a kind of longing that I'd rarely seen in a church of any kind.

"A Love that Forgives" was the title of the Sunday school lesson, and the verse that accompanied it had been Genesis 50:20: "...ye thought evil against me; but God meant it unto good, to bring to pass, as it is this day, to save much people alive."

The service, which had been unusually restrained, gradually began to heat up.

"You think God has forgotten about you!" Rev. Price said.

Yes, Lord.

"You've got trouble upon trouble!"

Mmmm, mmmm.

"But sometimes we got to wait on the Lord!"

Amen, Brother.

"Prison wasn't the perfect place!"

It sure wasn't.

"But it was the best place!"

Yes it was!

"There are pit stops along the way," he said. He had slowed down a little, his voice quavering. "But whatever stop you're at now...it's not the last stop!"

Preach it!

"God's gonna teach you something!"

That's right...he will!

Then he cited Genesis 39:21, in which God was with Joseph in prison and "shewed him mercy, and gave him favour in the sight of the keeper of the prison."

"God was there in the midst of violence..." Rev. Price said. "He was in control during slavery, Reconstruction, World War One, World War Two, the Freedom Rides.... He's still in control!"

Yes he is.

"Only God," he said, "can move you from obstacle to opportunity, from the cotton fields... to the White House!"

And this time there was applause.

When it ebbed, Rev. Price slowed down again. After all, this was 2013, not 1963. It was a time for reflection and reconciliation. "What would you do if you had the chance to pay people back with the love that forgives? That's the reason we're here today. Black and white together. God turned around evil and turned it into good. He specializes in that. He's a God that's able to do all these things. Give me enemies so I can... forgive them, for they know not what they do."

He was a hard act to follow. I think Jesse Jackson knew it immediately. His remarks were brief and vague, but one line was just rhetorical enough to convince the crowd that he was, indeed, Jesse Jackson: "We couldn't stop the crucifixion," he said, "and *they* couldn't stop the resurrection."

After the service, in a final tribute to the girls, a wreath was laid by the memorial outside the church next to the door to the Sunday school classrooms and the bathroom where the girls had been brushing their hair and straightening their sashes when the bomb went off.

Then the bell tolled.

Afterward Jim, Colin, and I went for Sunday dinner at Sweet Tea, a cafeteria-style restaurant on Birmingham's Southside that specialized in southern cooking. Earlier that morning I'd been afraid we wouldn't be able to get into the restaurant, what with the thousands packing the streets of downtown Birmingham, but since they never showed up the line wasn't bad, just the usual Sunday after-church crowd. In front of us in line was a beer-bellied guy in a crimson University of Alabama T-shirt and his wife, and in front of them was a young black couple who must have just come from church, perhaps even from the 16th Street Baptist. Nothing out of the ordinary was going on until another young black couple entered the restaurant and joined the couple already in line. The first couple had clearly been saving places for the new couple, and all four seemed to be wonderful young people just happy to have Sunday dinner together after church. The guy in the red T-shirt wasn't happy about this.

"What do you people think you're doing?" he said.

"Pardon me?" one of the young black women said.

"I said what the hell do you think you're doing?"

"Whoa, whoa," one of the black guys said with a smile. "We're not doing anything. We were just saving places for our friends so we could all sit together."

"And I guess you weren't thinking about the people like us who were already in line."

For some reason the white guy in the red shirt assumed he was speaking for those of us behind him, but nobody else in line seemed to care. We'd all arrived about the same time, and the two black couples had come in not five minutes apart.

"I'm sorry, mister," the black guy said. "If it bothers you, we'll go to the back."

"Yeah, well, it does bother me, so sure, get to the back, where you belong."

"It's like the old days," whispered one of the elderly white men in line behind us, but his wife shushed him.

Jim and I motioned for the newly arrived black couple to get in front of us, for which they were grateful, but I knew what they were thinking, along with the rest of us, black or white, particularly the ones who were old enough to remember: Birmingham was still Birmingham.

A place is so often still a place.

12

The Feast of the Sacrifice

By late September 2013, three more Western journalists, Spaniards this time, had been kidnapped in northern Syria, and tensions in the town of Azaz had reached a crisis point when ISIS gunmen entered the hospital there. They'd come for a German doctor they accused of being an infidel and a spy. When hospital personnel refused to let them take him into custody, they opened fire, killing one of the patients at point-blank range. In the melee, the German doctor escaped.

ISIS then sent in reinforcements with heavy weapons, even tanks. They killed the head of the Free Syrian Army's Azaz press office and took dozens of prisoners from there and from the Azaz Media Center. I had no idea whether Anas, Wahid, and Nasir were still alive. The same was true of my friends Yusuf and Nabeel, who had taken me to Aleppo in March. None of them answered my calls or e-mails, and because of the kidnapping threat and the fighting between ISIS and the FSA, Turkey closed its border at Kilis, and most Western news organizations ordered their staff and stringers not to enter northern Syria at all.

A distinguished French journalist I'd met at the Antik Han Restaurant was particularly annoyed. He was champing at the bit to get back into Syria. "But what can I do?" he said. Instead, he'd hired Henri to drive him along the Turkish side of the border, looking primarily for human-interest stories. He understood the restriction, of course, since four of his countrymen had been kidnapped and held for months. But the end of Ramadan was approaching, and just as the beginning had been, the end would be marked by a spike in fighting, and the fighting could never be stopped unless the world took note of it. The Syrian civil war was too important, and tragic, a story to go unreported.

Ramadan always ends at sundown with Eid al-Adha, the Feast of the Sacrifice. Honoring Abraham, who had been willing to sacrifice his son Ishmael before God sent a ram in his place, it is one of the most important holidays of the Muslim year, but that morning a car bomb had exploded in the Syrian town of Darkush as worshippers were leaving the mosque there. Darkush was just across the Orontes River from Turkey. An early report from Reuters indicated that twenty-seven civilians had been killed, including one woman and three children, with the usual caveat that the toll could be expected to rise. The numbers that residents told us in Haji Pasha, on the Turkish side of the border, where the most seriously injured had been taken, were more than forty dead and more than one hundred injured.

Henri and I got within sight of Darkush not long after the blast. The town was made of white stone and looked like heaven above the gently swelling hills of olive groves, but the only way to get to it would have been to cross the bridge controlled by ISIS petroleum smugglers or to swim the Orontes. We counted the enormous trucks carrying the contraband petrol, a dozen or more in less than an hour, right under the nose of Turkish soldiers who were manning the border watchtowers and lounging in the foxholes a mile or two up the road. As we left the river, we were accosted by a scraggly group of young men, some even boys, who were serving as lookouts for the smugglers. They were armed with handguns and carried cell phones, and they were not at all happy to see us. When the leader of the group, the one brandishing his gun, started accusing us of being infidels, Henri broke into a blistering torrent of Arabic, which he later told me turned the tables on them by accusing them of being infidels. "You say we're not sons of the Father!" he told them. "Well, you're not the sons of the Father! We are! So get out of our way!"

It worked. "I'm glad you're Muslim," I said to him in the car.

"I'm not," he said. "I'm a Christian. I've already told you that, when we first met. Don't you remember?"

Now I did, but just barely.

By the time we got back to Antioch, residents were already slaughtering goats and lambs on the sidewalks and alleyways of the old city, roasting them on open fires, and sharing the plenty with their families and neighbors, particularly those most in need. This time, though, there was a chilling difference that probably went unnoticed in Antioch but most certainly did not in Syria. Because of the war, the chief Muslim cleric in Damascus had made a concession so that believers could participate in the festivities despite the widespread hunger of many and the imminent starvation of some. This time the cleric had issued a fatwa allowing Syrian Muslims to eat cats and dogs.

I didn't bring up that subject at the luncheon I attended the next day at the Antioch Protestant Church, which was pastored by a Methodist minister, Seongho (Yackup) Chang, who'd come to Antioch from South Korea in 2007. His Korean wife, Mary, had cooked the food, a lavish spread of Korean delicacies including kimchi and *mandu* dumplings, and it was one of the best meals I'd ever had. The luncheon, held at the church's Agape Café on long tables pushed together, was in honor of an American couple who were on a worldwide evangelism mission trip.

They were a very attractive couple, well-spoken and well-informed. The wife told me her husband had been a devil worshipper when she met him. I found that hard to believe. He looked like a high school science teacher, a nice guy with a good sense of humor. Those devil worshippers were a crafty lot, though.

The Americans and I quickly discovered that we had something in common. We'd both spent time in El Salvador during the eighties. In fact, our paths had practically crossed during the final guerrilla offensive in the capital, San Salvador, in 1989.

They had been helping to establish small Pentecostal churches wherever they went, forty-two in all, they said. During that time, three of the cars they used had been stolen. They found themselves at gunpoint many times. Once there was a grenade in their driveway. But the final guerrilla offensive caught them by surprise, as it did almost everybody else, including the U.S. government. The couple lived in the upscale neighborhood of Escalón, which wound up being the site of some of the fiercest fighting of the offensive. I found myself in Escalón, too, right after my friend Melita's mother, who lived across the street from one of the presidential residences, went outside and told the guerrillas on top of her roof to stop shooting like that and come down. They did.

The American woman, meanwhile, saw a man shot and killed in her front yard. "His feet flew up in the air," she said, "and his shoes came off." She shuddered with the memory. Then she confided that she and her husband had told their two sons to run into the back bedroom, but the boys wanted to stay. "They were excited about being in a real war," she said.

The missionary couple, like most other Americans in San Salvador, were finally ordered to evacuate. They were probably sequestered in the Sheraton hotel, waiting for a flight out, at the very moment I was landing in San Salvador on one of my final assignments during the war.

The Camino Real, where most of the international journalists stayed, was practically deserted when I arrived; the others had probably headed to Berlin to cover the fall of the wall, or to Panama in anticipation of the U.S. invasion there. I watched the last of the fireworks in San Salvador, the tracer rounds and mortar flashes, from my room on the fourth floor of the hotel, and the next day took a cab to the scene of the massacre of the Jesuit priests, their housekeeper, and her daughter at the University of Central America. On the way, I got out of the cab to watch a city bus burn, torched by guerrillas, and then visited those poorer neighborhoods most affected by the fighting— Mejicanos and Zacamil—where most residents appeared to support the guerrillas and so were bombed and strafed by government aircraft.

Men who refused to fight alongside the guerrillas, though, like the father of a twelve-year-old girl I interviewed, were shot to death on the spot. And then, of course, there was Soyapango, the area pulverized by thousand-pound bombs. The sound of automatic-weapons fire continued in ravines hidden from view, ravines that I didn't go down, for reasons too obvious to explain. But on the street above, children dressed like angels and shepherds rode a mule-drawn cart through the town, scattering flower petals as they went.

When I told the American missionary wife that the good thing about the Salvadoran civil war was that the country was so small, we reporters could leave our hotel after a breakfast buffet, go talk to the army, then talk to the guerrillas, and return to the hotel in time for a hot shower and a meal, she was shocked. "You talked to the enemy?" she said.

"Why, yes," I said. "Both sides."

She turned to her husband. "Did you hear that?" she said. "He talked to the enemy!"

I shrugged, and he smiled. I think the former devil worshipper understood.

That was the week two British humanitarian aid workers, whom I'll call Leonora and Thomas, knocked on my door at Father Domenico's church. They knew I'd crossed over. They were expecting to do the same. They had worked for many years in crises all over the world, most notably in the aftermath of the massive 2005 earthquake in Pakistan that had killed more than 79,000 people.

Since they were also staying at the church, I asked about their religious affiliations or beliefs. Neither had any, but they were not unsympathetic to the Christians that they had served during famines and natural disasters. "The Kenyan Christians," Leonora said, "carry the happy/clappy stuff along with them because it gives them some relief. They don't have anything else. But I don't believe in any of it."

The Brits were interested in visiting the refugee camp called Atmeh, which was across the border from Reyhanlı, about a twenty-minute drive from Antioch. Once there, we went to the office of a humanitarian organization that gave Syrians living in Europe a place to stay when they returned to help their countrymen, particularly in the camps. And it was there, in the office, where we met the Syrian who would be Leonora and Thomas's translator, a big bear of a man named Omar Alkhani. Omar was articulate and self-assured, despite having been kidnapped by ISIS in August. He said he had just escaped from their underground prison in Aleppo, where he'd been held for weeks.

After we sat cross-legged on the floor to have tea, I scooted over closer to Omar so I could ask him privately what it had been like in that ISIS prison. He said it was beyond anything I could imagine, but he couldn't go into detail because there were still people there whom his captors would hurt if they found out he'd been talking. Then he and the Brits got into a heated discussion about their particular humanitarian project. Leonora and Thomas wanted to transport one of those massive shipping containers full of clothes, food, and medical supplies to Turkey via sea and then overland to Atmeh for distribution to the refugees. Once empty, the container, which had been wired, plumbed, and insulated, could be used as a clinic, office, or shelter. It sounded like a great idea to me, but Omar tried to direct the discussion elsewhere, to a water project of his own at a town deeper inside Syria. This project seemed not to interest the Brits, so he excused himself to smoke a cigarette on the balcony. The Brits continued their conversation with another Syrian named Elias. His English was not as good as Omar's, but he was patient and tenderhearted, especially for a man who had fought in both armies, first Bashar's and then the FSA.

I listened to their conversation a moment longer before I followed Omar onto the balcony, where he offered me a cigarette, then told me how difficult it had been for Syrian Sunnis in Reyhanlı after the twin car bombs had exploded in May. No matter whom the Turkish government blamed for the blasts, the Sunnis were afraid there would be reprisals against them. It didn't help when Turkey's prime minister, soon to be president, Erdoğan, said that the more than fifty dead had been Sunni when many had in fact been Alevi. His comment was a reminder of the rage Alevis harbored against a man who did not acknowledge that their form of Islam was a legitimate faith. After the bombings there were demonstrations, some violent, expressing Alevi fury in the street in front of the building where the humanitarian agency had its office.

"So we hung a huge Turkish flag from the railing of this balcony," Omar said. "We wanted everyone to think that we were loyal Turks, not Syrian troublemakers." As for conditions in the prison, he said his cellmate had been taken out and shot, and that he himself had been forced by guards to watch the beheading of a Shi'a believer.

We were both quiet for a moment, and then Omar confided in a low but matter-of-fact voice that one of the people still in the ISIS prison, the one who might be hurt if he said anything about conditions there, was his American wife. Her name was Kayla, and she was from Arizona. After this startling piece of news he began talking about a short documentary of his that had been shown in London ("Piccadilly Circus!" he said) and might be selected for inclusion in a film festival in Glasgow. I was a bit surprised that he would tell me about his wife and then segue into ruminations about his documentary's chances at a film festival. I felt as though I were missing something here, and didn't know whether I should believe him or not. If his American wife was really in an ISIS prison, why would he share that information with a perfect stranger like me and then immediately turn the conversation to the mundane?

When I asked if he'd like to visit America someday, he said no. When I asked if he had ever met, or would like to meet, his wife's family, he also said no, although I'd later find out that they regularly communicated with him via Skype. As we walked back inside, Omar continued to talk about the film, his work with an international news organization, and about the many other contacts he had among Western journalists. All he said to the Brits about his wife was that she was an American humanitarian aid worker and that she and he didn't watch news on television. They got all their information from the Internet or in person, and they were going to write a book about their experiences in Syria.

Again, I felt uneasy. Was this man seriously thinking about the book they were going to write when his wife was still in the hands of ISIS? Was he fantasizing about television cameras and public appearances? Agents? Movie rights? And if he had the chance, why wouldn't he want to go to Arizona and meet her family?

As for the journey across the border, Omar reminded us that today, Friday, was a holy day, so the trip would have to wait until tomorrow or the day after that. "You'll all have to say you're Syrians," he added. I took it as a joke. I wasn't about to pose as someone I wasn't. The idea didn't bother the Brits. They were so clearly impatient to cross, they didn't care what they had to pretend. Omar assured them that he was expecting a call from the security people there to find out exactly when the Brits could cross. In the meantime, he asked if there was anything in Reyhanlı we'd like to see. I suggested hospitals, particularly ones where we could talk to the patients, so he agreed to find out what he could do about that.

"Maybe in the morning," he said.

The next day Omar took us to three hospitals in Reyhanlı, including one he'd never visited before, and this one, unlike the other two—which were financed by Saudis or other wealthy donors from the Emirates—was clearly clandestine, unsanitary, and dark. The patients were men and boys who had been terribly injured. Some were missing eyes, jaws, or hobbled on metal crutches that creaked as they swayed. One of the medics said he understood that high-quality artificial limbs were expensive. He complained about the cheap ones provided by some aid organizations, items that lasted only a few months, and said that if the most severely injured patients could just get electric wheelchairs, it would help them immeasurably.

About that time, in the doorway to a corridor on my right, someone pushed a wheelchair into view. Tied into a sitting position with strips of bed linen was a pale young man without legs and with only one arm. In a whisper he said he was nineteen and from Homs, and that he'd been pulling guard duty at a corner in his neighborhood when a regime mortar round exploded. He was eager to talk, so I wanted to interview him further, especially since we had Omar there as a translator, but Leonora insisted that this was not what she and Thomas had come to the Turkish-Syrian border to do. They were here to take photos at the refugee camp where they intended to deliver the shipping container. The photos were needed for fund-raising purposes.

I told her that if I were directing a humanitarian aid organization, I wouldn't come this far just to take photos in order to raise money back in Great Britain.

"Yes," she said evenly, "but you're not the director of a humanitarian aid organization."

"No, I'm not." I pointed toward the guy in the wheelchair. "But why don't you just listen to his story? He wants people to know what he's been through and what it's like for him now."

By this time other staff members and patients had filled the room. They were gesturing wildly and insisting that Omar translate for them, while he was trying to calm and reassure them. This was all a misunderstanding, he seemed to be indicating. The ruckus ended when Leonora insisted we leave. She said something to the staff that indicated she would find somebody to come and assess their needs. The medics and patients didn't seem to buy that, though.

Back at the office, Omar said he thought he could finally get us across the border. I wanted to make sure who controlled Atmeh, though.

"ISIS controls Atmeh," he said. "But we probably won't even see them. If we do, you'll just have to pretend you're English or Scottish instead of American."

I told him I wasn't going to do that.

He smiled. "ISIS doesn't control the refugee camp. They just control the *town* of Atmeh."

"And that's *how* far away from the camp?"
"At least four kilometers."
"Yeah, well, thanks but no thanks."

So when Omar and the Brits eventually left for the border, I spent my time with Elias, the other Syrian in the office, the one who'd fought on both sides in the war. He told me how he'd slipped away from his regime unit and joined the FSA but became disillusioned with them because of the graft and corruption of their commanders, who rarely came to the battlefield and spent most of their time in Antioch with their rich wives and fancy cars.

Leonora, Thomas, and Omar got back sooner than we thought they would. They had been unable to cross the border, and Omar pulled me aside at one point to tell me the guards probably wouldn't let them in because of what had happened at that last hospital we'd gone to.

But to them he simply said, "We can try again tomorrow. There will be different guards there then."

As we were leaving the office a sixteen-year-old named Muhammad asked us to give him a ride home, and we agreed. In the course of that brief ride, he wanted to show us photographs on his cell phone. Two were of his father, who'd lost a leg when their house in Syria was bombed. The first looked as though it had been taken right after the blast. His father was lying in a heap in the rubble. You could see he'd been terribly injured below his waist, but the shot was unfocused and taken from a distance. Another body was lying behind his, a neighborhood boy, who Muhammad said had been killed. He skipped the next photo and went to the last, of his father bandaged and sitting more or less upright in a chair. And when Muhammad went back to the photo he'd skipped, I saw that it was the same neighborhood boy, washed and lying on a white sheet. His eyes were open and his face was turned to the side, serene, almost as if expecting something nice. But half of his torso had been peeled away, revealing his organs on that side, his lungs, liver, and intestines, like one of those plastic mannequins used in biology class, the kind with removable parts. Between this boy's legs was an explosion of blood, nothing but blood.

"You need to see these photos," I said to the Brits, but Thomas was driving and Leonora was busy trying to figure out the best route in order to get to the airport.

When we stopped in front of Muhammad's house, he invited us in for tea. He wanted us to meet his father, but Leonora said we were pressed for time. Maybe another day. So the boy bowed, put his hand to his head and heart, and simply said, "God bless you."

Back at the church, Leonora told me how she'd gotten into this business, if that's what you'd call it, of responding to humanitarian crises around the world. It started when she was a young woman on a sightseeing visit to the Far East. She had no idea that history would fall down on her. She was staying in Beijing, and her hotel happened to front a place called Tiananmen Square. The reservation had been made long before, of course, but Leonora was excited to see the student democracy movement flowering beneath her feet. She saw the Goddess of Liberty statue. She was there for the concert by Hou Dejian, one of the hundreds of thousands who rapturously celebrated what felt like the dawning of a new era of peace and liberty in their ancient nation. She couldn't understand a word of Mandarin, and few if any of the revelers around her knew a word of English, but it was as if language wasn't needed anymore. Freedom was all that mattered.

"You know the end of this story as well as I do," she said.

Leonora was there when the government loudspeakers announced the ultimatum to clear the square. The army was on its way. She went back to her room in the hotel, and from there she watched in horror the events that unfolded. She saw soldiers firing into the crowd; she saw hundreds mowed down by automatic weapons; she saw motorized vehicles crushing tents and lean-tos where people she'd just met were crouching in terror. At first she was paralyzed.

As a Westerner and a potential suspect as a provocateur, she feared she would not make it out of Beijing alive. But another young woman, who was from New Zealand and whom Leonora didn't know, took her under her wing. The New Zealander, who was part of a large tour group, had been told to go immediately to the airport, where the tour company had arranged an emergency flight out for the group members.

So she and Leonora left the hotel, and all their belongings, by a back exit, paid an exorbitant amount of money to a cabbie, and somehow made it to the airport. The New Zealander told the tour guides that they had to allow Leonora on the plane. They refused, but the girl kept insisting, until she finally said that if Leonora wasn't allowed to get on the plane, she wasn't going to board, either. That did the trick. The tour guides found Leonora a seat on that plane.

With that story, whatever had gone wrong between Leonora and me was completely healed. I had been in no position to pull out the righteousness card. The very reason I had come to the Turkish-Syrian border was to find the faith I'd lost in self-indulgence and, for lack of a better word, sin. To watch a pair of nonbelievers like Leonora and Thomas struggle with the same helplessness in the face of evil gave me hope that I might follow in their footsteps somewhere along the way. They were the heroes of my story, not me. They were the ones who were truly committed to the welfare of the Syrians who were suffering.

We talked a long time in that kitchen, took photos of one another, and I showed Leonora the ones I'd taken during my other trips to the region, particularly to Azaz and Aleppo. They were of men searching through their bombed-out neighborhoods for the remains of their wives and children, of a boy holding a kerchief to his mouth against the smell of death. They were of the blasted courtyard of the ancient Great Mosque of Aleppo, the bullet impacts on the walls and ceilings of the prayer hall where women could no longer pray. A light seemed to turn on in Leonora's head.

"If we're not able to cross the border tomorrow, do you think it might be possible for us to use some of your photos in our promotional materials, with proper credit to you, of course? We should probably try Lebanon next."

"Sure," I said.

Six months later, when she got to the Lebanese town of Arsal in the Bekaa Valley, al-Nusra and ISIS had just crossed the border, killing fifteen Lebanese soldiers and taking twenty soldiers and security men hostage, two of whom they later beheaded. In the melee, artillery shells and grenades had set fires that destroyed thirteen tent camps and killed nearly fifty civilians.

Leonora wrote that the fire had gone through the camps "like wind." "One of the Syrian team, Obidaa the medic, heard and saw people screaming for rescue from one of the burning camps," she continued, "but he couldn't help them. The gunfire was too fierce."

It was the worst spillover into Lebanon from the Syrian civil war, and Leonora's aid organization was the first on the scene. She met a father who'd lost two children in the fire. She saw seventy families living in nine of the remaining tents. Altogether, as many as ten thousand refugees lost everything. She had enough cash to find three water trucks and enough bread for around six hundred people, and then the shipping container arrived with ten tons of food, an ambulance, warm clothing, and medical supplies. The container itself would be converted into a clinic.

The substance of things hoped for.

13

Carrie Lawson

I'd see Omar Alkhani a second time before I went back to Texas for Christmas. He was sitting, his back to me, at a booth in the Liwan café. The man who sat across from him was wearing a steel-gray suit and looked American to me. I didn't want to disturb them, but when Omar happened to glance over his shoulder and saw me, he stood up, opening his arms, and gave me a big bear hug. Then he enthusiastically introduced me as his good American friend to the man in gray, whom Omar said worked at the Canadian embassy in Ankara.

The Canadian stood up and smiled as he gave me a quick once-over. Then we shook hands, and I stumbled over a thank-you for Canada's help . . . "you know, with the hostage situation." The Canadian, who must have been thirty years younger than me, looked confused.

"In Iran," I said.

"Oh, the movie. What was it called?" He appeared relieved.

"*Argo*," I said, and added, "I hope you can help us here."

At this his relief seemed to turn to concern.

Omar asked me to join them at the table, but I told him I should wait outside for Henri, who was taking me to the airport. Besides, two other men dressed in steel-gray suits had entered the hotel. Cursory introductions were made and I tried to excuse myself, but before I could leave, Omar's Canadian friend pressed his card into my hand and told me I should give him a call if I ever made it to Ankara. He'd like to talk to me there. We could meet for breakfast or lunch.

"When are you coming back to Turkey?" Omar asked me.

"January."

"Good, good. Don't forget to call me. I'll cook dinner for you. I'm a great cook." He reached into his pocket for a pen, but I said I already had his number.

"The Brits," I added.

He smiled, as if we were speaking in code. "Now, don't forget," he said.

I nodded, shouldered my backpack, and walked outside into the sun. I'd have to wait a while there for Henri, but I knew my staying in the café would have been awkward.

I assumed that the Canadian was acting in the interest of the United States to help bring Omar's wife home. But I also couldn't help but wonder if the Canadian's friendship with Omar wasn't a means of keeping tabs on Omar himself.

The minute Omar had told me, on that September day in Reyhanlı, about the kidnapping of his American wife, I'd thought of Carrie Lawson, a twenty-five-year-old woman who'd been kidnapped for ransom twenty-two years before in Alabama. At the time I was doing some stringing for the Atlanta bureau chief of the *New York Times*. My assignments mainly involved searching for court records in Birmingham or covering press conferences that he wasn't able to attend. I'd feed him the basic facts, and he'd either use them or not in articles he was working on.

One September afternoon in 1991, a Friday, I got a call from him as I waited in line to pick up my daughters at their school. He said there was an important news conference in Jasper, Alabama, that afternoon at four. It concerned a kidnapping case, and because the notice had been so short, he wouldn't be able to get over there to cover it. He asked if I could do it. He said if I did, I'd be reporting back to the national desk instead of to him, and if I did a really good job, they might even let me write the story.

I hadn't heard about any kidnapping, but I quickly called a neighbor to pick up the girls and drove to Jasper as fast as I could. The press conference was over by the time I got there. I could have kicked myself for not driving faster, but then I saw one man coming down the hall. I asked whether he had been at the press conference and if he had, what had gone on there.

He told me he'd been there, and reached into his pants pocket and pulled out a tiny tape cassette. "Here," he said, handing it to me.

"What's it about?" I asked.

"Just play it. You'll see."

I told him I didn't have a cassette player with me and tried to give it back, but he just smiled and said, "I don't need it now. There are plenty of others to go around."

When I got back to Birmingham, I listened to the cassette. The next day I returned to Jasper, and that night I wrote the following article, under the guiding hand of Paul Haskins, my assignment editor on the national desk. It was my first piece in the *New York Times*, and it carried my byline. More important than that, of course, was the subject of the story, the young woman who had been taken from her family by a ruthless man who probably had no intention of giving her back. That was when I discovered how rare kidnappings for ransom were in America and how dark was the place where the crime had occurred: my place, hardscrabble north Alabama, where coal and iron were not nearly as hard as the human heart.

JASPER JOURNAL
Familiar Voice Talks of Kidnapping

Jasper, Alabama
Sept. 19, 1991.

The four-lane highway into Jasper passes the Alabama Snake Farm; Wesley's Booby Trap, which advertises "Exotic Dancing"; and signs at service stations reminding motorists that it is dove season and that the new frog skin bags have just arrived.

The town itself, immaculate in the gold light of early fall, appears serene and untouched by tragedy, except for the marquee on a Baptist church, which reads, "Pray for the Safe Return of Carrie Lawson."

In the early morning hours of Wednesday, Sept. 11, 1991, Carrie Lawson, a 25-year-old recent graduate of the University of Alabama School of Law, was abducted from her home in the exclusive Heritage Hills neighborhood by a gunman in a ski mask, who the Federal Bureau of Investigation said was alone. He had ordered Carrie to bind her husband's hands, left him in the family's garage, and demanded a reported $300,000 for Carrie's return.

Two days later, the ransom was paid, but the kidnapper failed to keep his side of the bargain. Carrie Lawson has not been heard from since.

Although they do not know the identity of her kidnapper, some residents of this northwestern Alabama town say they recognize something in the kidnapper's voice, which they heard on an edited audio tape made public by the F.B.I. and played on local radio and television.

The voice sounds familiar to Stuart Upton, a childhood friend of the victim's husband, Earl Lawson Jr. It also sounds familiar to the Rev. David S. Wallace, the minister of Jasper's First United Methodist Church, where Earl and Carrie Lawson are high school youth counselors.

"I didn't recognize it as the voice of a particular person," Mr. Wallace added with emphasis. "I just mean it sounded like a familiar voice . . . somebody very painful to listen to."

In the tape made public Friday by the bureau, in which the kidnapper delivers instructions to Mrs. Lawson's husband, the voice is high-pitched and nasal and eerily solicitous. "Earl, you got the money. All right. Go up 69 highway to Cullman, you with me?"

It is a voice from a country deep and unsettled — peculiar, insular and violent.

It is a voice, almost everyone agrees, from around here.

• • •

As the seat of Walker County, Jasper is the largest town in a province of contradictions. Walker and its surroundings are among Alabama's richest in natural resources. Fortunes have been made in coal and timber here; clear cutting and unsightly strip mines have been the price.

Despite its scars, the region attracts more than its share of visitors. Nearby Smith Lake is arguably the loveliest piece of inland water in the state. And not far up State Highway 195 lie the nearly pristine 26,000 acres of the Sipsey Wilderness, the jewel of the Bankhead National Forest.

But to unsympathetic outsiders, Walker County calls to mind violent labor disputes, mining accidents, widespread boot-legging and the machinations of organized crime. It is a place with so many secrets that the search for Carrie Lawson has resulted in an unexpected harvest of stolen vehicles, marijuana fields, illegal whisky stills and the bodies of four missing persons, none of them hers.

"What keeps me going," said her husband, "is the fact that there hasn't been a single piece of evidence that she's been hurt."

On this fragile hope, Earl Lawson's world now turns.

Mr. Lawson and other family members initially offered a reward of $100,000 for information about his wife. Last Monday that grew to $400,000 from contributions by people in Jasper.

Almost every day since the public announcement of the kid-napping and ransom payment, 50 to 200 volunteers from the Jas-per area have fanned out from the First United Methodist Church to search designated areas of Walker and surrounding counties. In addition to cars, trucks and feet, volunteers have employed horses, all-terrain vehicles, helicopters and planes. They have been assisted by an F.B.I. liaison agent, Roy Long from Florence, Ala.

On a recent Saturday afternoon, carloads of volunteers drove north from Jasper into Winston County, to a spot on a dirt road *near the place where volunteers found Mr. Lawson's Ford Explorer about a week ago. A bloodhound named Blu is said to have reacted positively at this edge of a rock bluff near unincorporated Black Pond.*

A number of searchers set off on foot into the woods at a prudent distance from the dog, so as not to throw him off a possible scent. Earl Lawson waited on the dirt road with an F.B.I. agent and others for word of the search.

While a helicopter carrying Carrie Lawson's sister, Margaret, and their father, David Smith, hovered overhead, the searchers followed a logging road into a thick forest of oak and hickory. The territory had been covered before on foot, but perhaps not well enough. Gradually the logging road that had narrowed into a trail disappeared in briars and ferns.

Twenty minutes into the woods, the searchers paused at the lip of a massive gorge while the bloodhound repeated its lunging movement. The dog's handler, from a sheriff's department in Mississippi, struggled to hold the lead. He was convinced that the bloodhound was onto something, so agent Long suggested that four volunteers go down into the gorge, a box canyon with limestone outcroppings and vertical drops that one searcher estimated at over 100 feet.

The descent was circuitous and slow. At the bottom, the searchers, including Mr. Wallace, the Lawsons' minister, spread out but found nothing.

When Mr. Wallace returned from the woods near Black Pond, his entrance at the church signaled that the search of the gorge was over, with no news to report.

He did have a story to tell, though: "We asked for that dog to be sent down because we didn't want to go into this steep hole. Well, the dog got down there, and the hole was so steep, not even he could get back out....So we ended up having to pick that dog up and carry him out of there."

His infectious laughter started everyone in the room laugh-
ing, including Mrs. Lawson's father, David Smith. As the laugh-
ter trailed off, Mr. Smith shook his head and said, "In a time
like this, you just got to find something to laugh about."

Outside the church, the air was unseasonably cool. Some-
time later, a hunter's moon rose, enormous but flattened at
the top. Beneath it, the searchers had returned to their homes,
and the town of Jasper, for the time being anyway, continued to
hold its breath.

The reason the FBI had gone public by releasing the audiotape of
the kidnapper's demands was because they'd botched the delivery of
the ransom money. The kidnapper had instructed that the bags of cash,
roughly $300,000 of it, be thrown over a tall wooden fence and into a
culvert behind a gas station in Jasper. The bags contained marked
bills and transmitters whose signals could be tracked by helicopter.
But somehow, perhaps because the transmitters and trackers weren't
using the same radio frequency, the agents lost track of the kidnapper, who'd apparently just taken the bags of money and run.

About a week later the FBI went public with that tape of the ransom demand, and the kidnapper's voice was identified by Jasper
residents. His name was Jerry Bland, and he was in the coal business.
Police and FBI agents surrounded his house, searched his truck, and
found some of the ransom money. They then let him leave the house
to talk to his lawyer. While he did that, police searched the house
and found most of the rest of the money. They didn't recover any
guns, but soon after Bland returned to the house, police heard a gunshot. When they entered, they discovered his body. They also discovered an apparent suicide note in which Bland said that the marked
bills found in his car and house were not the proceeds from a kidnapping, but were the result of a drug deal gone bad.

By this time a female cousin of Jerry Bland had been arrested.
She acknowledged that she had dropped Bland off at the Lawson
home on the morning of the kidnapping and had been with Carrie

Lawson in the early stages of the crime, but that she had last seen her alive with Bland, although she couldn't, or wouldn't, give any information about where the police ought to be looking for Carrie. She'd later be convicted of kidnapping and sentenced to life in prison.

Paul Haskins, my editor on the national desk, was mystified by the whole chain of events. He couldn't understand why this nonentity Jerry Bland, who knew he was about to kill himself, would write a suicide note denying his role in the kidnapping of Carrie Lawson and would attribute the presence of the marked ransom bills to a drug deal gone bad.

"What's with this little Alabama town?" Paul asked me. "Is there something going on there that we need to take a closer look at?"

It was a rhetorical question, of course. I knew what he'd say next. "I want you to go up there and poke around in Jasper. I want you to do a piece about drug trafficking in Walker County, Alabama. See what you can find out."

So I did my best, and it was like lifting the lid on a barrel of poisonous snakes. Political corruption, drug running, and murder were all in the mix. I started hearing from hit men. Walker County was said to have the highest percentage of hit men per capita in the United States. A nightspot owner told me he knew the name of the Jasper policeman who had fired the shot that killed Jerry Bland but he couldn't tell me. Too dangerous.

"Go to the courthouse," he said. "Do some looking around. You'll find out."

I didn't find the name, but the information I did find in researching the article was enough to keep me up all night. Very little of the hard stuff found its way into the article — too hard to corroborate. I should have persisted but I was starting to get death threats, and my children were young. We lived in the woods on the way to Jasper. I didn't mind so much taking risks for myself, but not for them.

Carrie Lawson was never found. And twenty-two years later, Carrie's sister, Margaret, still believed that a third party must have been involved in the kidnapping plot. As did I.

14

New Year's Eve

By the time I got back to Texas for Christmas, Gary had been to the emergency room twice more but had not been admitted. My sessions with my therapist continued. I told her I didn't know what I was going to do about my brother. His funds were exhausted. His Social Security check was only enough to pay half of his assisted living cost. Medicaid wasn't an option until he went back into a nursing home, and even then, he might not be approved for it because on paper he still owned a house in Alabama. It was taking the bank forever to get the gears of foreclosure rolling. And there was no way he could move in with me. I'd come out of bankruptcy, but I had taken in Vicki when she came out to Texas. She was baby-sitting the grandchildren a whole lot, but she hadn't yet qualified for Social Security so I was paying rent and utilities on the place, in addition to financial obligations from the divorce. I also tried to help my daughters as I could. There was another problem now, though, something more serious than anything I'd encountered.

In Aleppo I'd lost any interest I had in living. I think my therapist was afraid I'd take action if and when she left town. She told me it was getting close to the time when I needed to go into the hospital. So I packed an overnight bag and kept it by my cot.

There's no reason to overdramatize what followed. I'd been through this scenario twenty years before. On the Friday I was scheduled to attend a Christmas party at the home of my favorite colleague at the university, I picked up the bag and told Vicki that I needed to go to the hospital. She drove me there. It was only six blocks away, but very cold and windy that day. In the emergency room I was asked whether I was a danger to myself or others. I gave the magic word, yes, and suddenly I was under lock and key in the acute psychiatric unit with the other lunatics.

Every day I gave my social history to a parade of residents, social workers, and psychiatrists. The lead psychiatrist put my brother atop the list of stressors and the war in Syria a distant third. When I said that I felt like I'd suffered an injury inside my head while in Aleppo, neither he nor anyone else ordered a CT scan. They did order EKGs, though, since I had often been told I had an irregular heartbeat. But other than that and the daily taking of vital signs, no attention was paid to my principal complaint, which was that I didn't want to live anymore because I was no longer afraid to die.

When they transferred me to the less acute unit for the last few days of my stay, it was like lounging about in a luxury hotel, although I had to attend group meetings all afternoon. Most of us at the meetings were drunks or drug addicts, or had been at one time in the past. The schizophrenics had to stay in their holes in the acute unit, four to a room, or the really bad cases, like a young patient named Elvis, in a barred and locked cell.

We fortunate few who were transferred to the less acute unit played gin rummy, or made macaroni necklaces, or painted Christmas cards to give to our families when we got out. I was briefly the king of the Wii bowling tournament, and when the week my health insurance company had ordained for this treatment came to an end, I got a prescription for a new antidepressant and my health insurance company got a bill for $40,000.

Forty thousand dollars for one week. That amount of money could have fed, clothed, and cared for all of those hundred patients at Pastor's Juárez asylum for four months at least. There the patients sang, danced, prayed, took long walks in the desert, fed each other, bathed each other, clipped each other's nails, and rocked each other to sleep. When I was an observer there for a week, the patients and staff had given me exactly what I'd needed. They'd reminded me of what faith looked like in war, where ordinary people, under threat of death, smuggled bread to their hungry neighbors, dressed each other's wounds, exposed themselves to sniper fire, and laid down their lives for both strangers and friends.

Forty thousand dollars. What kind of health care had that money bought me? Better care, at least, than the kind millions of injured and dying Syrians had received in a war that the American government was ignoring for yet another year, after promising to help the Syrian people depose Bashar al-Assad, the eye doctor turned dictator turned butcher, the architect of the worst humanitarian tragedy of our times. The scope of that betrayal boggles the mind.

And on New Year's Eve 2013, it was clear that the worldwide war against fascism, whether secular, like his, or religious, like that of ISIS, would continue unabated into the new year.

That night I was washing my clothes at the local laundromat in Lubbock when I thought I recognized a familiar face. She was putting her clothes into one of the dryers.

"Anastasia?" I asked.

She turned and said she thought she'd recognized me, although it had been a long time and she wasn't sure. She asked how I'd been. I said fine, but I was dreading the next question I had to ask, because she was the wife of a colleague of mine who'd been diagnosed with brain cancer five years before and had been given six to eighteen months to live. But I'd been on leave for much of that time, and I'd never checked to see how he was. I assumed he'd died, but I'd forgotten whether anybody had told me that, and if they had, I'd never gone to a memorial service or sent a note or said anything to Anastasia, who worked in another, distant part of the campus.

I think I must have uttered a generic question, maybe "How's it going?" or something like that.

"We're fine," she said. "Bryce is still a handful. He's cooking all the time, though. He's gotten good at it!" She surely recognized the astonishment on my face. "Yep, it just couldn't kill him. He was too ornery for that."

"My God," I said. "That's wonderful. I want to see him sometime. Would that be okay?"

"Sure. Why don't you come over tonight?" she said. "He'd love to see you. He'll talk your ears off. You don't mind that, do you?"

I shook my head. She finished getting her laundry out of the dryer and then wrote down their address and gave it to me. The house wasn't far, less than a mile. I said I'd be over as soon as my clothes dried. "No, on second thought," I said, "I'll leave them in the dryer and come with you."

She agreed, and I was soon walking into their living room toward a tall figure in a black hooded sweatshirt who turned around and gave me a big smile. "Dennis!" he said, and we embraced. Bryce had been one of the only men in academia I could tolerate. He was one of the best men I'd ever known, and I was so ashamed that I hadn't kept up with him. But he didn't seem to care. He began talking and didn't stop until I had to go get my clothes, which I brought back and jumped right into the conversation again. The dining room of his home was filled with religious art but he was not a believer, he made very clear to me from the start. What he was, he said, was a cook.

We tried all of his newest concoctions. He made me taste his favorite wine. He flicked a few light switches, and we went out into the backyard so he could show me his garden. Not much was in season at that point, but he showed me where everything would start coming up in the spring and mature in the summer and fall. He listed the dishes he would make with each of them, and by that time I was shivering so much he apologized and made me go back inside.

We talked about old grudges we had with our colleagues in the department and about current events, which he had followed very carefully, particularly those in the Middle East. He knew I'd been making trips to Syria, and he pumped me for every detail, which I was happy to give.

We settled into chairs at the dining room table, and he told me about each of the religious reproductions and figurines on the wall. There was also an old photo of him, not quite religious in the sense we normally think of the word. It was taken in the early seventies when he was a graduate assistant at a university in California and Anastasia had been one of his undergraduate students. In the photo Bryce has just swung out over the water, released his grip from the rope, and is making a perfect dive into a lake surrounded by willows and pines. His hair is as long as a girl's, and he's buck naked.

The three of us couldn't contain ourselves. They laughed at me, I laughed at him, Anastasia laughed at both of us, and their daughter came into the room and told us to be quiet, her dinosaur was going to sleep. We stayed up until two or three o'clock. It was the best New Year's Eve I'd ever had.

It was better than prayer, this living.

15

The Most Beautiful Girl in the World

It's late January 2014, and I'm back in Antioch, walking down a cobbled alleyway to get a bite to eat, when Henri comes running up and says, "Quick. Come with me. I want to show you the most beautiful girl in the world."

"What are you talking about?" I say.

"Hurry, before she gets away. She's at the Liwan."

"Who is she?"

"The most beautiful girl in the world, that's who!"

We get there in time for Henri to catch her before she walks up the stairs. He touches her elbow, and she turns. "See? What did I tell you?" he says to me.

"Tell who?" she says. "Tell what?" She is smiling broadly, and I see what Henri means. This woman's teeth and eyes are perfect, she has a mane of wavy, dark hair, and her body is as thin and finely tuned as that of a model or actress. She must be both, I conclude. I'm too embarrassed to speak, but Henri introduces us, and perhaps because I'm an American, and an old one at that, she asks if I'd like to sit and have a cup of tea. Henri winks at me and leaves us in peace.

"So you're a journalist?" she says.

I tell her I used to be, many years ago, but that I'm not doing hard news anymore. "I'm trying to find and restore my faith by coming to a war zone."

She frowns. "So it *is* about the war."

"Not exactly. It's about borders where religions and cultures collide. I'm not a war correspondent."

"Good. I can't stand war junkies. All they care about is booze, shooting smack, and getting laid. Believe me, I know about that last part. One of them came up to me at a party and said, 'We've just made a bet on who winds up in bed with you tonight.' Can you believe that?"

I shook my head, but I could believe that.

"I'm a combat videographer," she says, "so I've seen a lot of bad stuff, but it bores me to just watch somebody shoot a gun and then watch somebody else shoot back. I only do that kind of work so I can make money to support my charity."

I ask her what she's doing in Antioch. She says she's looking for information about a journalist friend of hers, a good man really, not like the others. He has disappeared, and she thinks he's been kidnapped by ISIS.

"Steve Sotloff?" I say.

Her eyes widen, her jaw literally drops. "How do you know that name? It's blacklisted. Nobody should know that name."

I tell her that I think I met one of the last men to see Sotloff before he disappeared. I tell her it was a fluke, an interview that some Norwegians were conducting about two teenagers who'd run away to join the jihadists. I happened to be with the Norwegians. I give Sabaah the name of the man they were interviewing, and then I tell her that I'm also looking for information about a hostage.

She asks who.

"Kayla Mueller," I say.

The most beautiful girl in the world is not familiar with the name, but she has contacts. She'll check around.

It's only much later that I will realize that this disclosure may have been risky. And at the time of this conversation, I had no idea that I would ever meet the hostage's parents.

I'll call the most beautiful girl in the world Sabaah, the Arabic word for "morning," because her mother is Syrian, a fact that accounts for her extraordinary complexion, her exuberant hair, and perhaps even the whiteness of her teeth, her generosity, her infectious laugh. She has indeed worked as a model and actress, but I think her beauty is something that transcends the superficial. I am drawn to her because of the path she is opening for me. Without formalizing an agreement, we decide our interests coincide. We're both focusing on the humanitarian dimensions of the war. She wants to go to Kilis, where in this second frostbitten winter since I've been coming to the region, tens of thousands of refugees are trying to flee the barrel-bombing of Aleppo by Bashar al-Assad's warplanes and helicopters. In the process, they're having to cross from rebel-held territory in Aleppo into regime-held territory in the northwestern suburbs of the city and then straight into the fierce battle being fought between the Free Syrian Army and ISIS for control of Azaz and the Syrian border crossing opposite Kilis. The border on the Turkish side is officially closed, but if the refugees can somehow make it across into Kilis, she wants to help them, and I want to watch her do just that. She's not a believer, but it sounds as though she might be a saint.

"I guess you heard about the actress and the dog," Henri says the next day. I figure he's about to tell me a joke, but no, no, he says this is real.

"You know the actress I'm talking about. She's staying at the Liwan."

"Oh, Sabaah."

"Of course," he says. "How many actresses do you think are staying there?"

I say okay, just tell me the story.

Henri says that when Sabaah first came to the Liwan, she wanted to borrow a puppy from the pet store next door so that she could sleep with it at night in her bed. She loves dogs, she said. The hotel said no way. In desperation, Sabaah decided she had to do something for that puppy. He whined and looked so hungry, so every morning she bought meat from the butcher shop down the street and took it to the pet store and gave it to the owner to give to the puppy.

"That was sweet of her," I say.

"No, but listen to the rest. The owner of the pet store told me he gives some of the meat to the puppy, but most of it he takes home for his family to eat! He has a wife and grandchildren to feed! Hollywood, you see? That's Hollywood for you!"

• • •

The first thing Sabaah and I had to get straight was that when she nodded, no matter where we were, we had to leave whatever place we were in, preferably by the back door. She had a stalker.

I asked if he was dangerous.

"Well, he says he loves me so much that he would kill for me."

That didn't sound good.

"Then he says he loves me so much that he would kill me!"

That sounded even worse. I asked what he looked like.

"Oh, you'll know him. He's dark, never smiling. He always has a sneer on his face. One time he tried to kiss me. In Syria! During a firefight!"

"What did you do?"

"I pushed him away. And you know what he did then?"

I asked what he'd done.

"He told the Free Syrian Army commanders that I was a spy for the regime! They kidnapped me, bound my hands and feet, gagged me so I couldn't scream, and threw me into the back of a pickup truck. They kept me for two weeks, did mock executions, everything. I finally persuaded them that he was crazy with jealousy and mad because I wouldn't let him kiss me, and they let me go. Then the same thing happened again. When they let me go that second time, I told him he would have to write a letter to every rebel commander he'd told these lies to and apologize for what he'd done."

"And he did?"

"He'd better have," she said, "or I'll kill him."

One night, as we were having tea in the Liwan café and Sabaah was coming back from the ladies' room, her face turned ashen, or as ashen as a Middle Eastern face can turn, and I knew immediately what I would see if I looked over my shoulder. She quickly took a scarf from the pocket of her cardigan and tied it under her chin in such a way that her face was barely visible.

"Don't look," she said. "Ignore him."

But she was already taking the turn at the reception desk so we could exit the back way. I got up and followed her, but quickly shot a glance backward. I wished I hadn't. There was no question which man she meant among those sitting at a table under a painting of an Antioch street scene. He was glowering at me. That's all I needed or wanted to know. On the sidewalk, we took a quick turn up an alleyway.

"Where are you staying now?" Sabaah asked. She was breathing hard.

"The Catholic church."

"Is it secure?"

"As secure as any place here. The rooms open onto courtyards that only the residents have keys for."

"What about the price?"

I told her I didn't think it could be beat.

"Do you think the priest would let me stay there?"

"I don't see why not. I told him I wasn't a Catholic, and he took one look at me and said I didn't look like I would cause any trouble."

"Will you go with me tomorrow to see him?"

"Sure," I said.

The next day Sabaah charmed Father Domenico, as she did every man I saw her talk to during our brief forays together. Her power had to do, of course, with her physical beauty, but it also had to do with her way of deflecting attention from that, pretending it didn't exist, and turning the conversation in a light, often comic way, toward the man she was addressing. Her tone was never snide or belittling, even when she was trying to get an extravagantly low price for a hotel room. Some might say she was a con. I wouldn't say that, not even in retrospect.

After she moved into her room at Father Domenico's church, she waited until she'd gotten word that her stalker, whose name was Faisal, had gone back into Syria alone, on assignment for an international media outlet. "He even tried to kill his brother," she said as an afterthought. We spent the next few days planning the trips we'd take, first to Kilis, where Sabaah would find refugees to interview, and then up to Gaziantep so I could talk to members of the Christian Armenian community there. Finally we intended to head along the Turkish-Syrian border almost all the way to Iraq, to visit ancient monasteries and see if we could find out more about a story first reported by an AP correspondent who'd written that Kurdish Muslims were protecting Syrian Christian refugees from being abducted, tortured, and killed by ISIS. This sounded to me like the substance of things hoped for.

We planned these trips at Özhut, a coffee, tea, and pastry shop just a short walk across the Orontes from the main plaza of the city. It had fabulous Internet service, large windows overlooking the bridge and river, and a smoking section separated by a glass wall from the rest of the café, a particular enticement for many of the journalists, chain smokers who couldn't light up in any other indoor café. The place teemed with them and their fixers, and since Sabaah almost never ate anything but cake (seriously), it was a perfect place to have lunch in the nonsmoking section and plot our next moves.

We rented a car from a nearby agency, and the night before we left we toasted our new friendship with a glass of red wine at a table in Barudi, the restaurant and bar across the street from the Liwan. The music was soft, a wistful American country number, and although the bar was crowded, we had a room to ourselves. People would glance through the glass door and then decide against disturbing us. They probably mistook us for a father and daughter on a very special night out.

Sabaah said she'd gotten us a great translator. He lived in Kilis, and he was an inventor. He'd invented a robotic nurse.

"You're kidding me," I said. "I know that guy!"

"His English is perfect," she said.

"Yeah, I know. He followed me into the Hotel Istanbul before my first trip into Aleppo, offering his services, but I didn't take him seriously. I thought he was nuts. There's really a robotic nurse?"

"Yes," she said. "I've read all about it. He's always busy working on it, but he said he'd translate for me as a favor."

That called for another toast. She programmed her camera to take a photo of us there, and we went back to Father Domenico's church after that glass of red wine, full of our own sweet selves.

• • •

The next morning, though, Sabaah had bad news. The inventor had to back out of translating for us. Unforeseen problems with the robotic nurse. I asked her what we were going to do.

"I know this doesn't make any sense," she said, "but it's all I could think of. Faisal."

"No," I said.

"He's back from Syria, and he can do it. He wants to do it, he's a good translator, and he's dependable because he loves me."

Shit, I thought, you're kidding me. But I figured I didn't have anything to fear as long as he didn't cause her to veer off into a ravine.

Fortunately, Sabaah did all the talking on the road, and it was all about Faisal's treachery that had almost gotten her killed. "Did you write every commander you told those lies to?"

He nodded.

She said she didn't believe him. "I want to see a copy of every one."

He nodded again.

"I love you," he said.

"I know. Stop playing with my hair."

When we stopped for gas or to go to the bathroom, Faisal would find a place to buy flowers or one of those little ladybug cakes Sabaah so loved. Next day was Valentine's Day, after all. Really.

And from Antioch to Kilis, that's how it went, so predictable and unchanging that I actually fell asleep in the backseat. Sabaah would tell me later that Faisal liked me. I'm sure he saw I was no competition for him. The only competition he had was from Sabaah herself, and that would be impossible to overcome. In time I would start to secretly root for him, but that wouldn't happen until I was sure he didn't want to kill me.

When we got to Kilis, Sabaah wanted to get an establishing shot of the city from its highest point overlooking downtown and the distant Syrian hills and plains. The spot was directly underneath the walls and barbed wire of an enormous estate. We hadn't been there five minutes before a security guard pulled up and told us to go back to wherever we'd come from. Sabaah explained we weren't going to take video of the estate. The cameras would be focused only on the city below.

"We're not on private property here, are we?" she said coquettishly.

The guard took a deep breath, got back into his car, and drove away. A few minutes later the police arrived.

"I'll handle this," Sabaah said.

One of the officers understood enough English that he could give the others the information Sabaah was feeding him: that we were from a magazine and television channel in Great Britain that focused on undiscovered travel destinations of particular beauty.

"Journalists?" he asked.

"No, no," she said. "Travel writers, and he's our translator. Why? Is something happening around here?"

When the first officer told the others, they looked as though they couldn't believe it. But she was one hell of an actress. "Am I missing something?" She smiled. "Really, I need to know if something bad is happening here."

"Passports," the officer said.

"Our readers and viewers have to be notified in advance if there's trouble brewing in the destinations we select. From up here, everything looks so calm."

"Syrian?" the officer said when he'd gotten to Faisal's identification card, which we knew to be counterfeit and a bad reproduction. He'd told us on the way to Kilis that he'd intended to get a better one.

"Officer," Sabaah said, "do you happen to know of a restaurant near here where we could have lunch?"

The officer looked up from Faisal's fake ID. "The police station."

Faisal and I glanced at one another, but Sabaah kept her cool. "Is the food good there?"

"Yes," the officer said as he handed back Faisal's card. "Your article. When will it come out?"

"The summer issue, but it's only available in England." She frowned as though that were such a rotten shame.

• • •

We figured the policeman was kidding about good food at the police station, but we followed signs to the station anyway, and behold, it was on the ground floor of a luxury hotel under construction. There were tennis courts and a swimming pool out back. We couldn't process this. The Kilis police owned a hotel? We encountered no problems getting into the facility although we were warned by policemen at the front desk not to take any photographs. To the right of the desk was the entrance to a large, spotless restaurant with white tablecloths and silverware in paper envelopes stamped with the emblem and name of the Kilis police department. The food was excellent, and the joy we got e-mailing our friends to tell them we were eating lunch at a Turkish police station was enormous.

The rest of the day and well into the night was spent on the opposite side of town, as different from the luxury police hotel as a place could be. At the border, Syrian refugees were streaming across by foot with duffels on their heads and children on their backs. They didn't look as though they were relieved to be escaping a war. They looked as though they were in a windstorm, a tornado or hurricane, with no shelter to run to and no strength to run even if there had been one. Once they had made it into Turkey, though, there were plenty of taxis to take them to the bus station downtown. I don't know how they paid their fares, possibly with clothes or blankets they'd brought with them, personal items, a promise of money. In town the bus station was crowded with families trying to find transportation to anywhere but there. Bread lines had been started for the children by Hiba, a humanitarian medical relief organization, and blankets were distributed by a London-based organization in a campaign called Keep Syria Warm. As night descended, though, it was clear that hundreds would be sleeping on the streets of Kilis in subfreezing weather. They huddled in alleyways against the wind, lying on top of one another to conserve body heat.

The lucky ones who were able to find an unheated empty shop or storage unit crammed themselves into it, often twenty or thirty of them in a twelve-by-sixteen-foot space. Sabaah went from family to family, asking what they needed. If it was bread, she sent Faisal to the corner store. If it was transportation, she'd go through her contacts via Twitter, e-mail, or text message, and try to line rides up. Places to stay? Medicine? She'd do what she could. She had contact information for thousands of people through her charity. She made sure an elderly one-legged diabetic was able to get his insulin, and this was no easy matter in a place like Kilis, where services of every kind were strained and where resentment simmered over the sheer numbers of Syrians showing up with such extreme needs.

Occasionally when Faisal and I would lose her in the dark alleyways of the city, Faisal would start to panic. Whatever his flaws, I believe he did love her, and one time when we'd just about given up hope, a curly-haired child ran up smiling and asked if we were looking for the lady with the camera. "Follow me!" she said with a laugh, and we found Sabaah in a smoky apartment sitting cross-legged on the floor with the men while the women chattered away in the kitchen. She simply ignored the Arabic insistence that women stay in their place. Once she showed me a photo of herself at a strategy planning session of rebel commanders. Many of them were obviously unhappy to have a woman attending such an event, but her friend, the highest-ranking member of the group, had insisted that she be there. His disappearance in a firefight a few months before the trip to Kilis had broken her heart, and wherever we went, she always asked if anyone had heard anything about him. She assumed the worst, because that's what the Syrian civil war was for her: the worst.

She hated the war, everything about it. She'd twice been in vehicles rolled over by the blasts of rocket-propelled grenades. She'd also found herself crouching in the back corner of a house when a bomb fell and the house literally disappeared all around her. Yes, she hated all that. But at one point that night in Kilis, we went to the border for some last shots of refugees crossing over. As Sabaah set up her tripod and attached the video camera, the sound of automatic-weapons fire rattled out from the Syrian side of the border, where

the Free Syrian Army was trying to drive ISIS out of Azaz and protect the stranded refugees there.

Sabaah turned and gave me the biggest smile I'd yet seen from
her. It was the smile I'd seen on the faces of other journalists when
they knew they were getting close to the action. No matter what they
said, why else would they be there, if not for the electricity of war?

We returned to one of those unheated rooms on one of those dismal
streets in Kilis, where two families, all women and children, sixteen
in all, were settling in for the night. They seemed happy to see us.
One of the girls had been the one who showed Faisal and me where
Sabaah had disappeared to earlier in the evening, and this girl's
mother offered us food, a single pomegranate, which we split three
ways. We let the children from both families borrow our cameras
and take photos of themselves, some posed but most candid and
wildly funny. I would later post photos of these two families online.
I called them "the lucky ones" because they had been able to flee the
barrel-bombing of Aleppo and were no longer sleeping on the streets
of Kilis. I wanted my friends to see them for what they were, not
victims, but warm, hospitable, and hopeful people. I didn't mention
a few critical details, including the fact that two of the girls, aged
seventeen and fourteen, were still missing; that the father of one of
the families hadn't been at home when the bombs struck and wasn't
able to flee to Turkey, so was probably still in Aleppo; and that the
father of the other family had a leg blown off by one of the bombs
and was fighting for his life in a hospital. Too many refugee images
are interchangeable: children fighting for places in bread lines,
infants with open sores, women and old people on long walks with
whatever belongings they can carry on their backs. I left my friends
with one moment, a girl who came outside that night, leaned against
the tin wall, and started crying. She couldn't stop. She didn't care
about the camera; she wanted me, she wanted all of us, to know.
And when she had finally gotten hold of her grief she smiled, raised
her fist, flexed her bicep, and yelled, "Strong!"

16

Heading East

F aisal made the trip only as far as Gaziantep, where we spent the night. He had other translating duties there, but he bought Sabaah more flowers and cake before we left Gaziantep on our journey east without him. He had been secretly videoing her with his own camera, and he would edit the footage, add a terribly sentimental soundtrack, and present it to her when she got back to Antioch. Nothing seemed to please Sabaah more than seeing herself on camera.

Our final destination on this trip was the Turkish border town of Nusaybin, about seventy-five miles from Iraq. Across the Syrian border at Nusaybin was Qamishli, site of the refugee camp where Kurdish Muslims were reportedly protecting Syriac Christians from ISIS. Along the way, we'd be crossing the Euphrates.

The land between the Euphrates and Tigris had long been thought of as the birthplace of civilization, but the excavation of Göbekli Tepe, which began in 1963, suggested that the ten-thousand-year-old site was not only the first place where wheat had been domesticated, but that it was "the oldest religious site ever discovered." This religion, according to the man who discovered it, Klaus Schmidt, was one of death. And in the prophecy of Habakkuk, a minor Old Testament prophet, this was the land destined to be swept over by a locust of peoples, the Chaldeans. Many centuries later their neighbors and descendants, the Babylonians, would become the Aramaic-speaking Syriac Christians murdered by the Ottomans and Kurds during the great genocides of the early twentieth century.

At the Syriac Orthodox Church of the Forty Martyrs in Mardin, we found no evidence of paranoia or bitterness about their sad history. Perhaps that had more to do with the church as a tourist attraction than it did with a short memory on the part of the Syriac Christians. Mardin's status as one of the oldest inhabited places on earth, in addition to its extraordinary setting on a shiplike mountain topped by a ninth-century fort, seemed to guarantee that it couldn't be sullied by the political and religious crises of modern times. But the same could also have been said about Aleppo or Hama or the mountain town of Kassab in Syria. Before the war, that is.

Outside town, Deyrulzafaran, the fifth-century monastery built on a site used by ancient sun worshippers, was also more museum than sanctuary. There was no trace, no mention of the deadly friction between Islam and Christianity in the monastery gift shop. But at the second and grander monastery, Mor Gabriel, outside the town of Midyat, hardly anything was said that wasn't about that friction. Founded in 397, Mor Gabriel was arguably the oldest, and also one of the largest and most beautiful monasteries in the world. It was also one of the most miraculous, having been named for a seventh-century Syriac bishop who, according to legend, had brought four dead people back to life.

When Sabaah and I visited Mor Gabriel, the current archbishop told us that journalists didn't know anything about anything. Then he turned us over to his English-speaking assistant, a man who had heard nothing about Kurdish Muslims protecting Christians in the refugee camp at Qamishli. The assistant did, however, give us a history of the many horrors that Turkish Muslims had inflicted on Christians, from the genocide during World War I to the crimes of recent years, including allusions to the following: the shooting death of a Catholic priest in Trabzon, a city on the Black Sea coast, in 2006; the stabbing death and possible beheading of a Catholic bishop in İskenderun, not far from Antioch, in 2010; an attack against a French Canadian priest in the northeastern city of Samsun;

and the stabbing of a priest in İzmir and of another priest and monk with a kebab knife in a Catholic monastery in Mersin, all around the same time.

The worst, of course, was the torture and killing of three Christians at a book publishing company in the nearby city of Malatya on Easter Sunday 2007. He didn't linger on this crime, but according to an article on the website *Christian Today,* the torture lasted for three hours and included "disembowelment, emasculation, slicing open of various organs," hundreds of stab wounds, and then the final slitting of throats and near decapitations. There were plenty of things that had happened at Midyat, too, he said, including an angry mob that had marched three kilometers from the newer Muslim side of the city into the older and smaller Christian side before they were finally stopped by police. This was in direct reaction to cartoons in Danish and other European newspapers depicting the prophet Muhammad, strictly taboo in Islamic culture.

We were exhausted by the end of the assistant's monologue and thankful when he stopped and invited us to dinner with the archbishop and a host of elegantly dressed men. We were not allowed to sit at their table, of course, but at a tiny one in a corner of the room, and that was fine with us. When we left the monastery, we couldn't help but notice the cars now parked in the lot—the newest and priciest I'd ever seen at one time in one place.

Next day, the drive to Nusaybin, that Turkish town opposite Syrian Qamishli, was uneventful. It had started to drizzle by the time we arrived, and it was evident that we wouldn't be crossing. The Turkish army had a substantial presence there, and the warning signs on the fences made it clear that if we got too close to them we'd be shot, because this was an actual war zone. Not only were Syrian rebels fighting Bashar's forces on the other side of the border, but Free Syrian Army forces were fighting those of ISIS and sometimes those of al-Nusra, depending on whether al-Nusra was fighting ISIS at the moment or in league with them. Muddying the water even more was the fact that the Turkish army had been trying to quash a rebellion by Kurdish separatists for more than thirty years, with few cessations of hostilities along the way, and Nusaybin was the heart of Kurdish rebel territory. The United States, Turkey, the European Union, and NATO all considered the PKK, the Kurdistan Workers' Party, a terrorist organization. Theoretically, fighting between the Turkish army and the PKK could erupt at any moment in Nusaybin.

On the Syrian side, only a mile away, there was also a Kurd fighting force, the Peshmerga, mainly Iraqi Kurds whom the United States and its allies supported in spite of the fact that it cast its lot with the Syrian government. There was also a Syrian equivalent of the PKK called the PYD (Democratic Union Party) with an armed wing, the YPG. The PYD, too, was Kurdish, but where its sympathies lay in all this madness, other than with its titular link to the PKK, was something of a mystery to everyone, even to my acquaintance Hugh Pope, director of the Turkey/Cyprus Project of the International Crisis Group and the Western world's most astute expert on Turkey, who concluded that the PYD and YPG were likely to support Assad rather than any of the revolutionary forces.

This is all a way of saying that our trip to Nusaybin, Turkey, was nearly as nerve-racking as a trip into Syria. It had the feel of an American Wild West town, or Chicago during Prohibition, a place where every neighborhood, every street, seemed to be under the control of a different criminal family and about to explode. We were only a two-and-a-half-hour drive from Iraq—yet another troubled border in an inflamed and unpredictable part of the world.

Sabaah had an intuitive feel for the ethnic and political character of each neighborhood, so when we parked the car and started walking in the rain in order to find anyone who could speak English well enough to translate for us, she made all the right turns, avoiding the streets that might be hostile, and when nobody who met the English-speaking criterion turned up, she stopped at an outdoor produce stand and bought two kilos of tomatoes (she had asked for two tomatoes, but the exact order got lost in translation). The young man at the stand gladly showed us the way to a restaurant where he thought someone might speak English. Its owner and staff had just the man: the English teacher at the local school. So we sat and drank tea until school let out, but when the teacher arrived it was clear that his English was not much better than our Arabic, so we wound up leaving Nusaybin and driving almost all night at breakneck speed back to Antioch. We took the Turkish equivalent of a superhighway this time, unaware that our speeds were being electronically monitored and that the speeding tickets would be added to our car rental bill. We were also unaccustomed to Turkish safety standards where highways were being repaired. Apparently there were no such standards, and we each almost lost control of our vehicle trying to avoid catastrophes at unlighted, unmarked work sites.

The next morning there was good news and bad. The good news was that Omar Alkhani wanted us to come to dinner at the apartment of his cousin in Reyhanlı. The bad news was that he'd just returned from Aleppo, where he'd again been held by ISIS. They'd stolen his video equipment, his cell phone, passport, ID, and money.

I was eager to see what Sabaah thought of Omar, but I didn't give her a reading of my own. This was a social call, a chance to visit, and it was a fine one, full of laughter and good stories, only occasionally punctuated by the tragedies of war that had brought us together, the kidnapping of the aid workers and journalists and their welfare. Omar had now been twice imprisoned by ISIS, he said, the first time on August 4, along with Kayla and a few others. One of the people who had tortured him then was the head of security for ISIS, a Moroccan or Tunisian. "Somebody told me the Moroccan guy was gone for a few days, so I volunteered to help move some equipment and then went upstairs and told the whole story to a judge. He gave me papers to let me go free."

The second time he was taken prisoner was when he'd gone to Aleppo with members of an international media outlet. This time his captors moved him between prisons, the worst in what was called Industrial City, where they took prisoners outside to execute them. It was unclear to me how he'd gotten out of ISIS custody the second time.

When he asked Sabaah and me why we were there, Sabaah reminded him that we were there because he had invited us.

Omar was an incredible photographer, and he told Sabaah he'd decided to try his luck as a filmmaker. He throught his first short documentary was very good and showed it to us. It was vivid and dark, a man smoking a cigarette, his features unrecognizable, occa- sionally interspersed with frightening documentary footage of death and destruction in the Ghouta region of Damascus.

Another documentary was on the table in the treatment stage. He said he just needed to do some interviews. The third would be based on dreams he'd had in prison. "You don't know whether they're dreams or reality. Sometimes I know they're dreams. Sometimes they're dreams inside of dreams." His dream now, he said, was to hit the big time with a good full-length feature by the time he was seventy.

"You don't have to be Martin Scorsese," he said with a smile.

Omar's cousin had also been imprisoned and tortured, but by the Assad regime. His dream now was to go abroad to school. His Eng- lish was incredible, and since his chosen field was information tech- nology, I knew he wouldn't have trouble finding a school that would accept him.

The four of us had a fine meal together, and only occasionally did I wonder whether something was amiss. It had to do with the lure of the international film festivals and the ease with which Omar seemed to be able to talk to his wife in prison. He said they talked every week. "She's okay," he said.

"I don't want to torture myself," he added. "I put my life at risk to bring her back. The professional negotiators don't care. They only care about the foreign fighters inside."

He said he'd been to the American consulate in Adana and was embarrassed when they frisked him. "I was married to an American," he said. "I just didn't have the papers to prove it."

In the course of the evening I asked Omar if Kayla's parents might be willing to talk to me, solely about the primary object of my interest, in other words, faith. He said he would ask them.

Sabaah and Omar talked briefly about her friend Steve Sotloff. Omar said he and Sotloff had been in the same prison. "He was all right," Omar said.

Sabaah said that Steve didn't talk much, that everybody would rush to Jim Foley. She suggested that Omar speak with Barak Barfi, a Middle Eastern scholar and one of Steve's closest friends. Omar bristled. "I don't want to speak with Barak," he said.

But Sabaah said it was important that they talk to each other.

At some point we received news of a car bombing in the refugee camp at Bab al-Salameh, the Syrian crossing opposite Kilis, an explosion that had killed at least five and injured many more. Children were among the casualties.

"You can't trust anybody," Omar said.

"I don't trust him." These were the first words out of Sabaah's mouth after we said goodbye to Omar and his cousin and got into the car to go back to Father Domenico's church.

Why, she wondered, had Omar told us that ISIS had taken his video camera, a very expensive one like hers, when he brought one out after dinner to compare with hers? He could have bought another one, of course. She couldn't understand why he was so vehement about not talking to Barak Barfi, the Middle Eastern scholar and longtime friend of Steven Sotloff. She thought Barfi might have information to share about the hostages, including his wife. And she said it was unlikely that Kayla and Omar had gotten married in Beirut, as he claimed, because she wasn't Muslim.

Next morning she took me to the airport. She was going to return the car to the rental agency. The daily rental fee was on my credit card, and she'd take care of any other charges. Sabaah would soon be on her way to run in a marathon in order to raise money for her charity. What a woman. What a heart!

Within seventy-two hours I was driving from Lubbock to Prescott, Arizona, hoping to find the home of Kayla Mueller's parents. The address listed online was an old one, as were the telephone numbers. I didn't want to e-mail Omar to get the information. On the way to Arizona I thought about that Alabama kidnapping case I had covered twenty-two years before. When I would much later tell my older daughter where I had gone that spring weekend and why, she would say: "She was your Carrie Lawson, wasn't she, Dad?"

17

Going West

It had been a while since I'd headed due west, and I'd forgotten how the light changed on the reddish brown cliffs and plateaus of New Mexico before it shifted into multispectrum Arizona. I'd spent the night in Albuquerque and made it to Prescott the next day. Our family had flown into Phoenix one time and driven up to the Grand Canyon, where we almost froze to death, and the West had that feeling for me, anticipation and discomfort rolled into one.

I got to Prescott after dark, checked into a Motel 6, and ate a bowl of clam chowder at the restaurant next door. Then I got out the city maps I'd collected in order to find the location of the house where the Muellers had lived. I didn't know anybody in Prescott and wouldn't have called them if I had. I knew I had to keep what I was doing secret and at moments felt no better than a common criminal, invading a family's privacy at the very moment when catastrophe was driving them insane.

On the other hand I figured I'd never find them at all, but I had to give it a try. The next morning I picked an easy target, Mr. Mueller's business, Preferred Auto Body. Prescott is a compact little city laid out on a grid, and as long as you know which way is north and which way is south, you've got a chance of not getting lost. Now, that's in the city center, with the restaurants and saloons and real estate agencies crowded around the county courthouse square. Finding N. Washington, where the body shop was located, proved a little difficult. I think I didn't want to find it, because if I did I'd have to walk inside and ask to speak to Mr. Mueller, and I had no idea what he might do to me in that setting. He certainly wouldn't have told anybody there about Kayla's predicament yet, but I worried he

190

might either quietly call the police at my approach or hit me in the face, and why not?

Fortunately, the business was closed on Saturday. I breathed a sigh of relief, went back to my room, thought about checking out and heading back to Lubbock, but then got out the map and tried to piece together where the Muellers' former residence might be. It was out in the country, or suburban country, I guess, farther than I expected. I missed the turnoff onto the dead-end two-lane that would take me by their house and had to double back.

The exterior was tasteful, with a view of a valley that seemed to stretch forever under a cloudless sky, but for all its natural beauty, the place appeared deserted. There were no cars in the driveway, and the shrubs and limbs of small trees had been cut back precipitously, as though they'd been allowed to run riot for a time and had only recently been pruned, perhaps just enough to not draw the attention of passersby. The grounds looked like those of a household in distress, an imminent foreclosure or white sale, a sudden move to another town where nobody knew the owners and to which they would leave no forwarding address.

I knocked twice and waited, then knocked twice again. To my surprise, the door opened. A middle-aged man appeared, tall and handsome. I knew he was Carl Mueller; I'd seen his photograph in an article in the local paper that had to do with an outreach program to young women. I told him my name. He appeared stunned. Omar had told me that he and his wife would be willing to talk to me, but I saw now that Carl hadn't anticipated that I would try to visit so soon.

He invited me inside, where he and his wife were in the middle of dinner. There was the sound of small dogs barking. He said they would have to talk about whether they wanted to sit down with me. He asked me to wait in the living room, where there were photos of Kayla in various parts of the world, surrounded by appreciative villagers. I knew for a fact that this was a family that helped people in need, a characteristic that Kayla had inherited from her parents, along with their good name.

There were other photos as well, but I didn't know who the people in them were. If her parents agreed to speak with me, I wasn't going to ask. I'm sure they wanted no information released as long as she was alive, not even Kayla's age, gender, or the fact that there was another American hostage under ISIS's control. I knew the Muellers must be undergoing a grieving process even though Kayla was still alive, and I told myself I would try not to further complicate their anguish.

When Carl came back, he said that my showing up unannounced had distressed them, and that they needed more time to consider my request. He said he'd call me the next day with their decision.

The next day was a Sunday. I wasn't expecting a call, but it came. Carl said that, after much discussion, he and Marsha had decided to talk to me. When I asked where we should meet, he said at their home. When I asked what time, he said anytime. So I left immediately for their house; I was afraid they'd change their minds. Perhaps it would have been better if they had, because I didn't know what kind of solace I could have offered them.

When I got there, Carl let me in again. He directed me to a couch. He and Marsha both sat in chairs. She was lovely in the way of heroines who have suffered or are suffering, but whose strength rather than their frailty is the first thing we notice about them. Carl was subdued.

They said they thought I was a preacher, and I explained that I wasn't, just a guy who was trying to write a book about faith as it's defined in the first verse of Hebrews 11. The verse was familiar to both of them. They asked about a movie based on one of my books, so I knew they'd Googled me. I told them the book had been under a film option for many years, but that nothing had come of it and probably never would. The question threw me a little, though. They didn't know me, so I couldn't blame them for being suspicious.

I told them they could trust me. I continued talking about my career, my travels in Central America, and my obsession with a kidnapping twenty-three years before back in Alabama.

• • •

I told the Muellers about Carrie Lawson, the whole story, in order to explain why I was so interested in Kayla's plight. I'd seen how easy it was for even the best of America's agencies to fail in its efforts to save a life, and I had two primary questions related to that aspect of their situation: First, I asked if they trusted the people in the U.S. government who were helping them with their case. They said they hadn't gotten much help from any government officials. The next question I asked was whether they trusted Omar. I could tell the question gave them pause. They glanced at one another, but I didn't know exactly what that meant.

They asked me about the woman I'd been working alongside. I explained about Sabaah's charity and her experience as a conflict journalist. I suppose Omar had mentioned her to them. I told them they should get in touch with her.

I wanted to ask them about their church. And this led into my most important question: "How have you managed to hold up under all this?"

Carl explained that his family had a Lutheran background and that his grandfather was a minister, but that he and his wife now considered themselves Baptist.

"We used to be active in our church," he said, "but we don't go there anymore."

"Churches are made by man," Marsha added.

"We've confided in a few Christian friends," Carl said, "but some people just tune out in despair. We have our health, though, in spite of losing a lot of weight. And we have each other. And we have God."

I had thought I knew something about tragedy until this man opened his door and I looked into his face. Nobody I'd ever known had been where he and Marsha were then, with the exception of Carrie Lawson's parents, but even their plight offered a better chance of resolution. At least there had been a ransom demand, and it had been paid. The child of these parents was in the hands of the worst terrorist organization in the world; there had been no ransom demand; and even if there had been, the U.S. government wouldn't allow it to be paid. America didn't negotiate with terrorists. As though Jerry Bland in Alabama wasn't one.

But still, the Muellers believed in signs. They were always on the lookout for them. "I don't believe in coincidence," Marsha said, "and when you know God, you just keep growing and growing." She said that Kayla had probably studied religion because of that.

Carl said that throughout this ordeal, he and his wife had learned a lot about Islam and Sharia law. "That's part of the reason we don't go to church anymore. A lot of what goes on in church these days is just people telling about their personal relationships with God."

Marsha looked as though she might be on the verge of tears, but she collected herself. "God lets us see different things at different times. Some good people have shown up."

Carl looked up at the ceiling, trying to get the verse right: "For where two or three are gathered in my name," he said, "there am I in the midst of them."

Then Marsha remembered one of those signs they'd been talking about. "He saw a sign," she said as she turned to Carl. "Go ahead. Tell him."

His hands were on his knees. He looked at them. If he had stood up, I might have been afraid of him, he had that kind of strength. Leaning over his knees he seemed defenseless, but when he finally straightened his shoulders and back, he told me what his wife wanted me to hear. He had been behind a truck one day at a stop-light. He doesn't remember, if he ever knew, what kind of business the truck belonged to, but the sign on the back of the truck said, "We have found Kayla." Carl had returned home ecstatic. It was a sign, but of what, they could not be sure. They looked at me as though they wondered whether I might be a sign.

I wanted to tell them I wasn't. But I didn't know yet. Anything was possible. Nothing could be ruled out. We were in the middle of a mystery. What we did agree on was the verse in Matthew that Carl had just recited, and how it applied to us: "For where two or three are gathered together in my name, there am I in the midst of them." And that's when Marsha truly did tear up and said, "All we have is God."

I didn't want to leave, but I knew I should. I told them that if Kayla were returned to them, that would be the substance of things hoped for. I felt that such an event would certainly be faith in action.

What I didn't tell the Muellers, but probably suggested with my first questions, was that I didn't trust Omar any more than Sabaah did. He seemed too preoccupied with other things—his career, his films, the book he intended to write. I also didn't tell them about Omar's friend from the Canadian embassy. He'd told me he wanted to have lunch with me someday.

But that wouldn't happen until after I'd gone back to Antioch for the final time. I wanted to go into Syria again, and before I'd left to find the Muellers I'd seen the *Los Angeles Times* Beirut bureau chief at the Liwan. I asked him whether the border at Kilis was open, and who was in control of Azaz.

He said the border was open and ISIS was in control of Azaz. I said if I'd known that, I would have stuck around a while longer.

"Are you out of your mind?"

"You said the border was open and that the FSA was in control of Azaz."

"No. I said ISIS was in control, not the FSA!" And he shook his head as though he'd seen plenty of my kind before—dilettantes, adrenaline junkies.

A month later I'm in Texas writing checks and discover I can't sign my name. I know what my name is, I just can't sign it. I give a guest lecture at the university about something other than my current project, but I have to leave without answering questions from the class. It's as though I'm coming back from Aleppo, and that afternoon, while attending a retirement reception for two of my colleagues, I stumble into them. My friend Jill takes my arm, asks me what's wrong. I tell her I don't know. I can't walk up stairs. She has to help me up the stairs to my office to get my things, and then to the elevator and out to the parking deck.

"You need to go to the emergency room," she says.

"I'm fine."

"No, really, you need to go."

"If it gets worse I will."

"I'm serious about this. At least call your doctor."

"Sure," I say. "That's a good idea. I will."

She walks to her own car, and I get into mine.

But I don't call, not at first. I sit in my car, unsure whether I can handle traffic or find my way home. It's why I went to the emergency room in December and told the doctors that something had broken inside my head. I don't want to wind up in the psych unit again, but finally I make the call. It's after office hours. I leave a message describing my symptoms, then slowly drive the eight blocks home. By the time I get there the doctor on call has left a reply. He says the symptoms I've described are very serious and I should go to the emergency room immediately.

At the emergency room they do a CT scan, and a doctor comes in and tells me I have a large pool of blood on my brain and that the neurosurgeons are going to have go in and do something about it.

The neurosurgeons ask the same series of questions:

Were you in an automobile accident?

Did somebody hit you in the head with a baseball bat?

Did you fall down a flight of stairs?

I answer no to those questions, but I tell them I was in Aleppo, Syria, where there's a war going on, and I think an explosion might have caused a minor injury that has since become acute.

Forty-eight hours later, they're opening my skull and draining the pool of blood, a subdural hematoma that otherwise might have killed me.

18

Layla and the Wolf

I'll huff and I'll puff and I'll blow your house down.
                                                    —*The Wolf*

L ess than a month after the brain surgery I was back in Antioch.
    I hadn't yet had the postoperative appointment with my Lub-
bock surgeon nor met my Lubbock neurologist. He happened to be
from Aleppo. When I did ultimately see him, he would run through
the same questions I'd gotten from the doctors who'd read my CT
scan and the neurosurgeons when they'd first examined me:

Were you in an automobile accident?

Did somebody hit you in the head with a baseball bat?

Did you fall down a flight of stairs?

And then he looked up from his paperwork, smiled, and said,
"Was there an explosion?"

I nodded. When I told him which one I thought it was, the one as
I was coming out of the Old City, the loudest blast I'd ever heard but
the one that nobody else seemed to pay any attention to, he lay his
paperwork aside and stood up. "I imagine they're used to it," he said.
"Well, let's have a look at you."

That first morning back at Father Domenico's church I attended
Mass, something I had neglected to do on my most recent trips, and
it was there that something peculiar happened to me. I was the only
person in attendance, so I was sure that when Father Domenico

walked in, clothed in his robe and stole, he would acknowledge me but then return to his quarters.

Instead, he went through the liturgy exactly as I'd seen him do it before. He washed his hands, took the bread and wine to the front of the chapel, bowed, kissed the altar, read the appropriate words in a language I couldn't understand, sang at all the appropriate moments, and then put a little water in the cup of wine, swirled it around, dipped a piece of bread in it, and ate that bread and drank from that cup after holding it high above his head.

That's when I realized I'd been crying the whole time. More than I'd ever cried except for the day my father died.

Father Domenico didn't seem to notice as he bowed before the altar, folded the cloth that had covered the cup of wine, and stored it and the other sacred objects on a shelf. But before he left the chapel and returned to his quarters, he looked ever so slightly in my direction and smiled.

What was on my mind at that moment was the verse the Muellers and I had been talking about at the end of my visit with them. It was from Matthew 18:20: "For where two or three are gathered together in my name, there am I in the midst of them."

Father Domenico and I never talked about that morning Mass. There was no need.

The next, and final, time I went to Mass, I met two Westerners who wanted me to meet some Syrian artists who were opposed to the regime and had been going back to Syria not to fight, but to bring in art supplies and put them into the hands of children in what was left of the towns in rebel-held territory.

"For therapy or something?" I asked.

"No, just because the children like to draw and paint, and they don't have the materials to do that."

So they introduced me to the Syrian artists, and we all met at Asia one night and had what for me was a raucous good time. The Syrian director of the project struck me as a little reserved at first.

The other Syrian was a dancer and puppeteer, and therefore not reserved at all.

The director, whom I'll call Qasim, finally loosened up after telling me that he'd been a tank commander in the regime army. He'd been responsible for three tanks, including his own. All three were destroyed or disabled in battle. He was the only survivor, so he took the opportunity to slip away from the battlefield and defect to the Free Syrian Army. But after becoming disillusioned with what he said were corrupt rebel commanders, a story I'd heard numerous times by then, he'd left for Turkey, where he stayed for a while in a refugee camp built solely for defecting officers. I'd seen it on the outskirts of Hacıpaşa. It had its own town-sized water tower, mosque, and individual houses, all behind a concrete wall too high to scale. Qasim said that most of the officers there were generals, and he'd started resenting the way the superior officers treated the lower-ranking ones.

"I mean, we weren't in the war anymore," he said. "We weren't even in Syria anymore."

So he left the camp, traveled back and forth between Turkey and Syria trying to find a way to help the children, and then came upon the idea of the art supplies.

"Everybody thinks that in a war, the children draw only images of violence—warplanes, tanks, dead people on the ground. But most of the children I've met want to draw the things that would interest any child, anywhere: their families and friends; their homes and schools; animals, flowers, trees; and skies filled with clouds, sunsets, and rainbows. Sometimes they draw the faces of movie or TV stars. We have television in Syria, you know."

"The point is, we're not there to teach them how to draw," the dancer added. "We're there to give them the means to do it."

We'd finished our beer by then and were contemplating whether to order another when someone, probably the dancer, had the idea of using one of the empty bottles to play Truth or Dare. I'm not sure the Europeans knew what that was, but if they didn't, they soon found out. *Have you ever had sex with a woman?* The bottle rolled. *Kissed a man?* Rolled. *Looked in somebody's window when they didn't know you were doing it?* Rolled. The questions began to get more trivial or outlandish, the answers more or less believable, until the dancer finally said: "Ask me if I've ever killed a man."

No one said anything.

"Go on, ask me. Ask me if I've ever killed a man."

Qasim relented. "Okay. Have you ever killed a man?"

"Yes."

The dancer was still smiling, and it was time to go home for the night.

And then the friend of Omar's, that diplomat from the Canadian embassy, let me know he was in town. We arranged to have breakfast at the Liwan restaurant, and he chose a table far from the others. It was easy to get to the subject at hand. I figured he wanted to know about my meeting with Kayla's parents, so I told him that I'd asked two questions: whether they trusted Omar, and how they were enduring what they were going through.

"What made you ask about their trusting Omar?" the diplomat said.

I told him about the circumstances of my meeting Omar and how surprised I was that he would immediately reveal to a complete stranger the fact that his wife was being held by ISIS and then turn the conversation toward his documentary and its chances at various international film competitions.

The diplomat agreed that it was remarkable that Omar had been trying, and was able, to get on with his life in spite of all this. He said that if it were his wife, he'd probably be out of his mind and unable to think about anything else.

"Right."

Then I mentioned the possibility of a rescue mission. The diplomat said that would be a very difficult thing to do.

"What about black ops?" I said. "Isn't that what they're for?"

He said yes, and then we were silent for a while, until he reiterated how difficult a rescue operation would be. Altogether, the conversation was pleasant enough and covered a number of subjects, including my time in El Salvador decades before and the botched FBI ransom drop in the Carrie Lawson case back in Alabama. He listed the places he'd been posted, and talked about his previous career as a semiprofessional athlete.

I later saw Omar and the Canadian at Özhut. They had seated themselves at a table near mine and were sharing an intimate conversation. Omar was laughing at something the Canadian had said, but then the Canadian saw me and suggested to Omar that they move to a table in another part of the café. That's when I knew that no matter how cordial my conversation with the Canadian had been, my access to information about Kayla Mueller was over now, a feeling confirmed when I got a message from Omar telling me that he didn't want to talk to me on this trip. He was upset that I'd asked the Muellers if they trusted him, and he said that I'd shared some of his "private things" with them. I didn't want to argue with him, and I told him I'd admired his work and hoped she'd be returned to him and her family. What I left unsaid was that I didn't know what private things he was talking about, but I thought, and still do, that he shouldn't have been keeping things from her parents, particularly if he was sharing them with strangers like me.

What I discovered in Antioch on this last trip was an even more heightened sense of impending doom. I met humanitarian aid workers who had been going to Raqqa and Deir al-Zour, for instance, cities that were now totally under the control of ISIS. When I asked how many people the medical supplies had reached, one of the aid workers, an American from New England, said he didn't know because all the supplies had been stolen by ISIS.

The Czech security man for the organization, who'd done similar work in Somalia and other perilous places, said I was worth a million dollars. At first I was flattered, until I realized that he was talking about my value as a hostage.

The level of frustration with the United Nations was palpable. Even the best-run relief agencies seemed to be flailing about. There was infighting and confusion. One German woman with a high security clearance was having trouble mapping the fighting in northern Syria so that aid convoys would have safe passage to deliver supplies. The battle lines, when there were such things, were too fluid. In some places, al-Nusra was cooperating with ISIS. In others, the two factions were murdering one another. The various bands of more secular fighters were hopelessly fragmented and on the verge of disappearing entirely.

And the war's carnage was accelerating. The year 2014 would ultimately prove to be the deadliest of the war so far. The total number of dead during the conflict would stand at between 200,000 and 250,000 by year's end, with a million more injured. Four million refugees would have fled to adjoining countries. Seven million Syrians would be internally displaced. Half the population would be in need of humanitarian aid. And the children I'd visited who had been burned and otherwise disfigured were the most tragic reminders that what for commanders might have been dots on a topo map had been—even were, barely—small, habitable worlds where families had eaten and slept and dreamed.

The Westerners who had been working on the children's art project had gone back to their home countries. But Qasim, the dancer, and a musician who played the *nay,* a bamboo wind instrument, had not yet given up hope. When the war first started and they had no one to fear but Bashar al-Assad, they had established what amounted to an art center for children in the home of the dancer's grandfather. In fact, they called it "Home." They said they got used to being bombed. At the sound of planes or helicopters, they and the children just headed for cover. It almost became a game.

But when ISIS moved in and took over the town, fear came not only from the sky, but from every street corner, every alleyway. There was a punishment for every infraction, no matter how minor. If a woman plucked her eyebrows, she'd be taken to prison, given eighty lashes. If they saw that a man had an injury, no matter what its source, they would accuse him of having fought with the Free

Syrian Army, and he'd be beheaded. Executions in the street became commonplace. But Qasim and his friends refused to give up hope, at least not when they'd escaped to Turkey. They began putting together a puppet show for the children called "Layla and the Wolf," a version of the Little Red Riding Hood folktale, but one in which the Wolf was a thinly-disguised Bashar al-Assad. They were performing it in refugee camps on the Turkish side of the border, and at schools, parks, and playgrounds that would allow it. The project gave them a way to avoid the final tragedy of a peaceful, democratic revolution stolen by jihadist thugs.

Before I headed back to the States, Qasim took me to Yayladağı, the first place my translator Henri had taken me in July of 2012. There, I'd seen the town of Kassab high in the mountains on the Syrian side of the border. Two years later it was no longer a regime-held town about to be liberated by moderate Free Syrian Army rebels, but rather a town pounded by regime artillery and aircraft in an unsuccessful attempt to beat back the much more radical al-Nusra fighters, who were linked to al-Qaeda and who would, in coming days, murder unarmed Christians in the streets, destroy precious artifacts, and burn churches and deface the walls of those they spared with hateful graffiti.

Qasim and I were eating with Syrian refugees, a former FSA fighter and his family in Yayladağı, when we heard the first blasts. We climbed a wooden ladder to the roof and looked toward what had once been that lovely Armenian town in the saddle between the two green ridges. An artillery shell from there had destroyed a mosque in Yayladağı a few days before, but who could possibly have known which side or faction had fired it? The number of radical jihadists in Syria, which had been fewer than 1,500 in January 2013, had morphed into a fighting force of more than 26,000 by January 2014. The dream of a free and democratic Syria was dead. It's not that America had turned its back on Syria. As the director of one medical facility put it to me bluntly: "America never even gave us a back to turn."

· · ·

Which brings me to the really hard part of this story.

On July 4, 2014, less than six weeks after I left Antioch and returned to the States, the U.S. military launched a clandestine raid to rescue American hostages held by ISIS. The rescue attempt failed because the hostages had been moved to a different location. But the public announcement of the raid was not made until August 20, one day after ISIS released a video showing the beheading of James Foley. This horror was followed by the beheadings of Steven Sotloff on September 2 and of Peter Kassig on November 16. Two British hostages, David Haines and Alan Henning, and two Japanese hostages, Haruna Yukawa and Kenji Goto, would also be murdered in this obscene and gutless way. Ransoms were demanded in each case but were not allowed, by our government, the British, or the Japanese, to be paid.

That left at least two Western hostages still under ISIS control: British journalist Peter Cantlie, who had been kidnapped along with James Foley on Thanksgiving Day 2012, and a twenty-six-year-old American woman whose name had not yet been released but whose captivity had been announced by her family through a spokesperson on August 22, 2014. At that time, ISIS was demanding a ransom of $6.6 million. The family spokesperson acknowledged that the woman hostage was a humanitarian aid worker but did not release her name or the circumstances of her kidnapping.

Five months later, President Obama's chief of staff accidentally mentioned the hostage's first name on television. Three weeks after that, ISIS released a video that purported to show them burning a Jordanian pilot to death, and Kayla's fate became increasingly dire.

The next Friday, February 6, 2015, ISIS issued a statement saying that the American, Kayla Mueller, had died. Her family held out hope over the weekend that the statement had been false, but on Tuesday, February 10, they and President Obama confirmed her death. ISIS claimed that Kayla had been killed in a Jordanian airstrike, but the American administration found that account highly

improbable. Months later we would learn that during her imprison-
ment she had been physically and sexually abused by her captors,
including Abu Bakr al-Baghdadi, the self-proclaimed caliph of what
he was calling the Islamic State. We would also find out that she
had befriended two of her fellow prisoners, young Yazidi sisters who
said, after their escape, that Kayla had mothered and protected
them, even passing up a chance to escape with them because her
presence as a Westerner might have put their lives in danger.

"Greater love hath no man than this," Jesus said, "that a man lay
down his life for his friends." (John 15:13)

My brother Gary, meanwhile, managed to step back from death's
door. Last month was his birthday, and I took him a card and a package of Peanut Butter Snickers, his favorite chocolate treat. I thought
I'd just be holding up the package and that he would never be able to
actually eat one of the bars, but when I walked into his room, he was
sitting up in bed and chowing down on barbecued chicken and
baked beans. He smiled up at me, and I dabbed the barbecue sauce
off his chin.

"Promise you'll take me back to Birmingham," he whispered.

"Of course I will," I lied.

I wanted to tell him that we can never go back to the past, a good
thing for the most part but a terrible thing for that part of the past
that included the lives of our mother and father, our brother and
sister, and the young woman we never knew, Kayla Mueller.

On a night soon after the confirmation of Kayla's death, I took a walk
with my dog down our dirt road in West Texas. The sun had set, but
the horizon was still a blood-red line. Above it, the moon was thin
and bowl shaped, hardly visible at all, and there was one very bright
star or planet above the moon. When I came back inside, I took out
my Texas stargazing book but was still unable to identify what that
light might be. Instead, I got online and saw that in Prescott, there
had been an outdoor memorial service honoring Kayla's life.

I don't plan on ever moving back to Birmingham or returning to the Turkish-Syrian border. I like these skies out here in West Texas, and tonight, as I'm writing this, my dog and I have just returned from our last walk before we go to bed. We walked much farther this time than usual, down that familiar dirt road between the cotton fields, and suddenly the stars all appeared on display out there—the Big Dipper, the Seven Sisters, even the faint constellation called Berenice's Hair.

It's the end of my three-year search for faith, but I'm still not sure whether there's a God or not. If there is, he must be as distant as those stars.

I can't deny the existence of faith, though. I've seen it in the eyes of children, my own and the ones I've met from El Salvador to Mexico to Syria. I believe that faith was once in my own eyes as well.

My favorite hymn when I was a child was called "Dwelling in Beulah Land," and I sang its chorus with what I can only describe as joy:

> *I'm living on the mountain, underneath a cloudless sky,*
> *I'm drinking at the fountain that never shall run dry;*
> *Oh, yes! I'm feasting on the manna from a bountiful supply,*
> *For I am dwelling in Beulah Land.*

Faith, as Saint Paul said in his letter to the Galatians, is a fruit of the Spirit, and a fruit is something tangible, life-sustaining. A gift. But I don't think the gift of faith comes from a church or a religion. I think it comes from the same source that life does, and that it first arrived in our consciousness as a conviction that life had meaning. We knew we hadn't invented ourselves, nor the garden in which we first woke up. We didn't have to kill ourselves, or someone else, in order to arrive in paradise. It was already there, all around us. All we had to do was keep ourselves from destroying it and reconcile ourselves to the truth that just as we would someday have to leave it, we'd just as surely leave a bit of it behind.

EPILOGUE

An epilogue is meant to be an ending. But even endings have to begin somewhere, and this particular one began on a day when I was walking to Father Domenico's from my favorite Antioch café and saw a young fair-haired woman with a backpack slung over one shoulder instead of both, a sure sign she was a journalist instead of a graduate student on holiday. She was, in fact, a twenty-seven-year-old journalist from Australia.

"Are you planning to cross into Syria?" I asked.

She nodded yes. "Why? Have you been in?"

I nodded.

"Where?"

"Aleppo."

She smiled. "That's where I'm going."

I begged her not to.

"Why not?"

"It's too dangerous."

"I'll be fine," she said, still smiling.

"I don't think you understand. Didn't you hear about the two London *Times* correspondents kidnapped the day before yesterday in Azaz?"

"Of course."

"They were tied up and thrown into the trunk of a car."

"But they were able to escape," she said with that infuriating smile.

"Yes, after one of them had been horribly beaten and shot twice in the leg. And they wouldn't have been able to escape at all if one of the jihadists hadn't helped free them out of the goodness of his heart."

"Well, they were double-crossed to begin with," she said. "I shouldn't have a problem with that sort of thing. I'll be going in with a team of Syrian doctors, and I'll be wearing Islamic garb. It's easier for Western women to go incognito into Syria than it is for men, you know. The only things I'll have to fear are those barrel bombs."

"Right, and you remember the Canadian photographer who was killed by a barrel bomb in Aleppo a few months ago?"

"Yes," she said. "I knew him. We met in Egypt, in fact shared a place for a while. His photos weren't selling, so he decided he'd have better luck if he went to Syria." Then after a pause, she said, "I don't guess he did."

"Okay, I give up," I said. "But I want you to have my cell number, and I insist you call me when you get back. How long do you expect to be in?"

"Maybe four days."

So we traded cell numbers, and I said, "Be safe."

"You, too. I'll tell you all about it."

I watched her walk down the alleyway, a perfectly fine young woman with that certain madness in her bones. It wasn't a suicidal impulse; I knew what one of those was like. This was the opposite, a desperation to live intensely so as not to die before we were dead.

I hoped to see the Australian again, but with a border like the one between Turkey and Syria, return was never a given, not even if you were in the company of Syrian doctors, not even if you were wearing a black abaya from head to toe. Not even if you were a humanitarian aid worker like Kayla Mueller whose only reason for being there had been to ease the suffering caused by war.

Kayla Mueller's final testimony was not about herself. It was about her family and what they'd done for her. In a letter to them smuggled out by one of her fellow prisoners, she wrote: "By your prayers I have felt tenderly cradled in free fall. I have been shown in darkness, light."

The text message from the Australian came four days after she'd crossed into Syria: "I made it back."

And when we later talked by phone, she said that upon reaching the Turkish side of the border, she'd gotten on her knees and kissed the ground.

ACKNOWLEDGMENTS

The facts and figures not the result of my own eyewitness, or that of individuals I interviewed, can be attributed to a number of important sources. The two murders that occurred in Juárez on Good Friday in April of 2012 were reported in *El Diario de El Paso* by staff. The discovery later that month of the remains of the young women in the desert outside the city was reported by staff in *El Diaro de Juárez*. The very best source of information about the violence in Juárez on a daily—sometimes hourly, sometimes minute-by-minute—basis is the online *Frontera List* compiled and administered by Molly Molloy.

I will forever be indebted to the late Chuck Bowden for his books and friendship, and to José Antonio Galván and the staff and patients of the Albergue Para Discapacitados in Juárez for hosting me during my time there.

The source to go to about Birmingham during the civil rights movement is without a doubt Diane McWhorter's Pulitzer Prize–winning volume *Carry Me Home,* a monumental work of literary journalism.

The violent ISIS takeover of Azaz, Syria, in September of 2013 was reported by Aymenn Jawad Al-Tamimi in a post entitled "Analyzing Events in Azaz—A Detailed Look at ISIS' Takeover." His analysis appeared on the Brown Moses Blog, October 9, 2013.

The most reliable figures about casualties during the Syrian civil war have come from the London-based Syrian Observatory for Human Rights, which has contacts on the ground in places where providing such information is itself a matter of life or death. Similar figures provided by the United Nations have generally been thought inadequate, although the United Nations High Commissioner for Refugees (UNHCR) is certainly the best source for refugee numbers.

Of the many articles I read before and during my journeys to the Middle East, the ones most useful to me were those from the *New York Times,* particularly its reporters C. J. Chivers, Ben Hubbard, and Anne Barnard; the *Washington Post's* Liz Sly; the *Los Angeles Times's* Patrick J. McDonnell; *The Guardian's* Martin Chulov; and the journalists from my favorite English-language newspaper in Turkey, *Today's Zaman.* No one knows more about the Turkish-Syrian border region than Hugh Pope, and any discussion of the American hostages in Syria and their families' attempts to rescue them must begin and end with the reporting of *The New Yorker's* Lawrence Wright.

Special thanks go to the people in the book who, for security reasons, remain unnamed, and to my family, friends, students, and colleagues. All of you know who you are.

Special thanks, also, to my agent, Jennifer Lyons, for being my torchbearer in the dark world of twenty-first-century book publishing, and to my editor, John Parsley, for keeping me focused on the spiritual nature of our project and gently encouraging me to work harder than I've ever worked before.

My most profound thanks, though, go to Carl and Marsha Mueller for opening their home and hearts to me.

Please remember the Syrian people, not only the injured and the dead, but the ones still fighting to survive in Syria and abroad.

May the Judeo-Christian Jehovah, the Islamic Allah, and the unknown god hold us tenderly in their hands.

ABOUT THE AUTHOR

DENNIS COVINGTON is the author of two novels and three nonfiction books. His book *Salvation on Sand Mountain* was a National Book Award finalist, and his articles have been published in the *New York Times, Los Angeles Times Magazine, Lapham's Quarterly, Vogue,* and many other periodicals. He was born in Birmingham, Alabama, and earned a BA from the University of Virginia and an MFA from the Iowa Writers' Workshop, where he studied under Raymond Carver. He currently teaches creative writing at Texas Tech University.